Toilet Training Your Puppy

The Complete Guide for New Dog Owners

James Leung

Table of Contents

Introduction: Your New Puppy and You

You've just gotten a new puppy. Congratulations! No doubt you want to learn everything you can about puppies so that you and your new little friend can build a great relationship together. I'm sure you will have a lot of questions. Among them is likely regarding the tricky topic of toilet training your puppy.

You Can Do It—And So Can Your Puppy!

Puppies are eager to bond with their new owners just as much as the owners want to bond with their new puppies. Working together towards good toilet habits can be part of that bonding experience. It will give you both a sense of accomplishment and help ensure that your new relationship is off to a good start.

One of the major reasons that puppies are abandoned or left at shelters is that the puppy soils indoors. That's not the puppy's fault—it just hasn't been trained properly. You want to learn the proper way to train your puppy in order to prevent this unhappy scenario.

You may think that puppy toilet training is difficult. It doesn't need to be if you endeavor to learn more about puppies and the principles of effective toilet training. By putting that knowledge to use, you can enjoy better, faster success than if you tried to manage puppy toilet training without it. This book is the guide you need to accomplish puppy toilet training with the maximum of success and the minimum of stress. Following these suggestions will lead to a happy, rewarding relationship with your puppy.

So, if you're ready, let's begin!

Chapter 1: Puppy in the House!

Above: Welcoming a new addition to the family. A lifetime of love.

You've invited a new puppy into your house to live with you. But what does that really mean? For one thing, it means that you now have to share your home with another creature that has its own needs, wants, and opinions. This affects not only you, it includes your family, who will also need to learn how to live with and care for a puppy. Then there are other factors to consider. For instance, you may already have an adult dog or other pets that might not appreciate having a newcomer encroaching on their territory and routine. No need to worry—there are several steps you can take to make this transition as easy as possible for everyone involved.

One of the first and most important things you'll want to accomplish to help things go smoothly is toilet training your new puppy. Of course, you want to avoid the mess and smell that go with having an untrained puppy in your house. You also want that puppy to grow into a healthy, happy dog. Believe it or not, puppy toilet training is an important part of that process!

Adding a Puppy to the Family
Preparing for Arrival

Once you bring your new puppy home from the shelter, breeder, or pet store, that's when the fun begins. Naturally, your puppy will want to run, jump, and play which is fun. But it will also do its business where you don't want it to.

That's because young puppies have not yet figured out the behaviors that humans want them to have. That takes time, a certain level of maturity, and practice. In other words, puppies have to learn to be trained. Fortunately, they have a natural desire to be hygienic. The idea is for you to present options that the puppy can use to guide its decision-making about where it is okay to go, and where it is not.

All of the people in your household need to learn about puppy toilet training, whether they are family, roommates, significant others, and including the person who may be taking care of your puppy when you need to be gone. So, in a manner of speaking, all the people in a puppy's life need to be trained, too—to care for the puppy properly as well as help meet its toileting needs.

If you are fortunate enough to get a puppy from a breeder who has started the toilet training process, you may be able to move quickly past some of the earliest steps. If you have arranged for a dog-sitter or dog walker, he or she may already be familiar with the basics. But for most people, the task of training a new puppy falls to the person who brought the puppy home. The more you understand about your new puppy, the more successful toilet training will be. It is important for you and your family to keep in mind that toilet training is a process; results won't be instantaneous.

Some people will tell you that a puppy can be trained in seven days or less. While it is possible that some puppies may grasp the basics that quickly, for the most part they simply cannot physically accomplish it. A certain amount of both mental and physical maturity is required. It takes longer than a week for the puppy to be able to figure out what the owner wants it to do, and even longer to be able to do it. This is particularly true if you, the puppy's teacher, do not have a lot of experience with toilet training dogs. You will both be learning at the same time. Be prepared for both you and your puppy to make mistakes. And above all, be patient. Rushing the training can mean that owners may skip over some important steps, or have unrealistic expectations.

You need to follow some simple procedures and do so consistently so that your puppy is able to cooperate with you in achieving your shared goal. And it *is* a shared goal. Your new puppy wants to make you happy and it wants to be happy living with you. That can't happen if you are both upset about toilet training.

Let's take a look at what makes a puppy behave the way it does. This insight can really help you understand your relationship with your new puppy and make toilet training easier and more effective.

A Pup Grows Up

Puppies go through a predictable series of stages in their development. It's important for you to understand your puppy's developmental stage in order to choose the right time for toilet training. Different breeds of dogs develop at different rates. Smaller breeds, for example, mature more rapidly than larger breeds. You also need to manage your expectations of your puppy's development and behavior. Puppy training is not a "one size fits all" proposition. Just because your previous dog took only four months to be completely trained and accident-proof does not mean your new puppy will be the same.

Pre-Weaning

Ideally, you should not get a puppy before it is weaned and able to leave its mother. The puppy needs to have its mother take care of its feeding, growth, and development. Puppies are pretty helpless at birth—though not as helpless as human infants. Some of the first things they must learn are how to open their eyes, gain some muscular control, and progress to the point where they can begin to eat solid food. They will start to be able to eat solid food at about three to five weeks old, depending on their breed, and can be on a totally solid diet by eight weeks old. 'Solid' is a relative term here. At that age, dry food should be soaked in water or milk substitute until it absorbs the liquid and swells up.

Puppies at the age of three or four weeks are also learning from their littermates and their mother how to socialize with other puppies and how to play without hurting others, something you'll definitely want your puppy to know. Socializing with humans can also begin at this stage, though it's important for the puppy not to leave its mother completely until about eight weeks of age. Have all the members of your household be involved in socializing the puppy, as they will all be important parts of its life—and important partners in the process of toilet training.

The Puppy Starts to Learn

From about six to eight weeks old, puppies can begin learning things that will be necessary for the toilet training process. For example, they can learn their names, as well as how good it feels to receive praise and rewards from their owners. By eight weeks, they will have also learned to feel fear, so it's a good idea to get them used to noises they will be hearing around the house such as doorbells and vacuum cleaners. They will also need to get used to any other animals you have in the house such as other dogs or cats.

Your puppy will be developing a distinct personality—loving, calm, cuddly, independent, nervous, or clinging, for example. By the way you train your puppy, you can influence the kind of personality it will grow to have. Gentle treatment and positive interactions will help the puppy see you as a benevolent presence, the source of treats and positive feelings. This will be invaluable in the process of toilet training as well as simply living together happily with a puppy.

If you treat a puppy harshly with your words or actions, it can develop a distrustful or fearful personality. You may have seen a dog that cowers when people come near it. This is likely because the owner never socialized it when it was a puppy to expect kind behavior from human beings.

If the puppy will be interacting with dogs, other puppies, or any pets already in the household, it is important to make sure it is used to the presence of other animals. Just as you would acclimate the puppy to all the human members of its family, you should make sure that the puppy gets used to their presence and that, in turn, the other pets understand how to interact with the puppy and help in its training. Before your new puppy interacts with other puppies or dogs, it should get all its shots and vaccinations. Puppy health is important for successful toilet training; by making sure yours is properly vaccinated, you also help avoid the spread of any potential diseases. You also want to check it for fleas or other transmissible issues that can affect any of the other pets in the house.

Learning Its Place

During the first six months, your puppy will be learning its place in the wider world. That includes not only you, your family and other caretakers and other pets, but also strange dogs it may encounter, or other animals it may see.

Some people think that puppies are like wolves and have an alpha male who dominates the pack and gets all the best food, as well as the most mating opportunities. They advise that you become like the alpha male to your puppy. You may have even heard that you should dominate your new companion by wrestling it or gripping it tightly by the scruff of its neck. This premise is untrue and the action unnecessary. The studies that led to these philosophies involved wolves in captivity, not in the wild. In the unnatural conditions of a research study, the wolves developed dominance-based behaviors. It won't help you in training your puppy, so it's best to ignore this type of advice. Dominating your new puppy will only complicate matters and may lead to behavior issues later.

Rather than having an alpha male—or even an alpha female—wolves in the wild live in packs or families with a pack leader. The pack leader does not dominate the other dogs but, as the word suggests, leads them through learning the tasks of daily living. Not all female dogs are subservient to male dogs, either. The father and mother are both pack leaders to their family of developing puppies. They lead by being good role models.

You don't have to dominate your new puppy, but you should take on the role of a leader, protecting the puppy and teaching it what it needs to know to live safely and happily with you. And, of course, that includes toilet training. One of the first things that puppies learn from their pack leaders is not to soil in the spaces where they sleep and eat—their dens. The mother dog keeps the den clean and, when the pups are old enough, pushes them out of the den to do their toileting. This lesson is invaluable for beginning to toilet train your puppy. A little later, we'll explore how.

The Puppy as a 'Teenager'

If you try to toilet train a puppy too soon, it will not be mature enough to understand what you want it to do or even be able to follow the steps of a good training program. If you wait too long, the puppy may have developed bad habits that will be difficult to break.

Basic toilet training should begin soon after your pup comes home. You can start the journey when it is eight to ten weeks old. Will a young puppy make mistakes? Yes, lots! Patience and consistency will be necessary in order to get past that initial stage. In general, at six months or so, depending on the puppy's breed, toilet training should be fairly complete; at that age the pup is roughly equivalent to an adolescent human—a canine teenager—and is ready to start learning the "rules of the road," including solidifying its toilet training outside of any confined spaces.

Socialization is also important to instill early because your puppy will need to know how to interact comfortably with other human beings and animals that it will meet on its daily walks. Of course, if you train your puppy to toilet indoors on a potty pad, maybe at a designated spot on a convenient balcony, you won't have to worry much about this kind of socialization, except for introducing it to the people and other pets in your household. And remember that if you do take your puppy outdoors to go, your puppy needs to be comfortable with the surroundings. Try to find an environment without traffic noise or a lot of other activity, preferably one with some grassy vegetation. Some pups and dogs can be a bit shy about pooping, and will feel most comfortable having a shrub or other light cover for this purpose. Your puppy will show you what it prefers.

The "teen years" are when your puppy's personality will really begin to solidify and its toilet training progress to a reasonable level. Will your new friend become a cooperative, well-mannered dog? Or will it become a holy terror that reacts with fear and anger in every situation? Surprisingly, toilet training can have a lot to do with this aspect of puppy development.

Above: Creating a life-long friendship: A well-socialized puppy.

Physically speaking, by the age of approximately one year, your puppy will mature into an adult dog. This varies depending on how large of a breed it is and the individual puppy's level of maturity and physical or mental development. The giant breeds such as Saint Bernards take longer to reach this stage. Once your puppy is old enough to understand that you want it to control its bladder and bowels, it will progress more rapidly through the process of toilet training.

You'll need to reinforce its early toilet training for consistency. Although there will still be accidents, your puppy will work out what it needs to do to please you and will try its best to cooperate. In the meantime, enjoy your puppy. You may want to keep a log of its progress and see how your puppy is developing toward your training goal. You may even want to take photos of your puppy every week—or more often—and keep them with the log so you can remember its growing-up days.

Why Toilet Train?

Of course, you want to toilet train your puppy so that it won't soil the rugs and floors of your house or apartment. But training is necessary because puppies don't just naturally grow out of soiling. Though adult dogs encourage young pups to pee and poop outside their dens, they do not teach them to control their bladders and bowels. You won't be able to directly teach the puppy to control its bladder and bowels either. The puppy's ability to do that depends on its age and level of development and you will have to work within those limits. The puppy will gradually gain more control, so just be patient with it. Adjust your puppy's training schedule so that your plan corresponds to its stage of development.

Besides being an important aspect of life together with human beings, toilet training is also good for your puppy's development and health. If you supervise your puppy's toileting habits, you will likely notice any irregularities that are signs of health problems. Blood in the urine or stool, incontinence, or inability to defecate or urinate may indicate physical problems that need veterinary attention. In particular, diarrhea, which may be caused by eating something it should not, such as toxic plants like tulips and azaleas, or by internal parasites, can be detected early so that the appropriate steps can be taken to alleviate the problem.

FAQ: What Are My Puppy's Toileting Needs?

Your puppy needs to have a safe, clean place to take care of its toileting needs. It needs a regular schedule that allows it to relieve itself regularly. And it needs encouragement in order to meet your expectations. All these are important aspects of puppy toilet training.

You want your puppy to know when and where to relieve itself. Leaving the decision up to the puppy will not improve your relationship, even though it may seem like forcing a puppy to go against its natural instincts is mean. Human children have to be potty-trained too, and no one thinks that's unnatural or harmful. And puppies can be toilet trained much more quickly and easily than infants!

Your puppy's toileting needs will vary depending on the size of the dog. Small breeds of dogs have smaller bladders and will need to empty them more often. Fortunately all dogs, regardless of breed, can be toilet trained. Science has found that genetics has no effect on learning behaviors such as toilet training.

To determine a place for your puppy to meet its toileting needs, consider your own circumstances. Do you have a house with a fenced yard? It may be ideal to designate an area of that for puppy toileting, and concern yourself primarily with outdoor training. One significant benefit to outdoor training is that grass and green areas will help encourage your pup to do its business more quickly than in an artificial environment like pavement, or your floor!

Do you live in an apartment or a house with no yard? In that case, you will probably want to explore your neighborhood for convenient, acceptable places for your puppy to relieve itself—other than a neighbor's lawn. Another option is to select an area in the house and use toilet training pads or grass pads, especially if you have a convenient balcony your puppy can use for its toileting location. Indoor versus outdoor training methods are not mutually exclusive. When your pup is very young, if easy access to the outdoors is not available, you may opt for indoor training. As the pup matures, you can introduce outdoor training, as well.

Sometimes, due to an incomplete vaccination schedule or perhaps the owners' living circumstances do not provide a private outdoor space, it is advisable and necessary to first start toilet training indoors. Indoor training is also useful for times when either the puppy or its people can't go out due to the weather, safety issues, health concerns, and the like. Once mature, most dogs choose to keep their territory clean given the opportunity, whether it is indoors or out.

Regularly scheduled toilet times for your puppy are vital. Be realistic when setting times. What works for your schedule and, more importantly, the puppy's? Be consistent; don't skip a scheduled training time. Whether the location is inside or out, remember that the younger the puppy, the less control it has. Focus on timing for the first thing in the day, after feedings and any play periods, and last thing before bed. Take the puppy to its designated location at the scheduled times. If the puppy doesn't go right away, wait patiently for 15 or 20 minutes.

Because a puppy's bladder and bowels are not fully developed yet they will need to go out many times a day. They will need to go out more often in the early days after first coming home. They will simply not be able to "hold it" when they are very young. Only as the puppy grows and matures will it gradually be able to begin to meet your wishes and expectations. Expecting a puppy to learn at a very young age is not possible. You'll have to put up with messes until the puppy develops both physically and mentally.

Encouragement from you is also necessary. A puppy can't toilet train itself! You will need to provide an environment in which the puppy receives gentle, positive reinforcement for learning to perform its biological functions in an appropriate place and at an appropriate time. One way to ensure you are giving good positive reinforcement is to have a "puppy party" when the pup does what it is supposed to do. Celebrating success with happy tones, a happy expression, cuddles, and treats will tick all the boxes for the puppy, and create deep connections for positive behavior. Keep it gentle, though—you don't want to startle the pup and create a negative association with going in the right place!

The most important thing in toilet training a puppy is reasonable expectations. Toilet training is a process; as your puppy grows from week to week, its abilities will improve. It will grow both physically and mentally. The puppy's ability to problem-solve and make mental connections will increase over time—for example, its ability to associate praise and treats with the idea that it has pleased its owner with its behavior.

It's not the puppy's responsibility to figure out when and where to go. The owner is responsible for training and encouraging the puppy. The process can start when the puppy is still young, but it *is* a process. Until the puppy is a 'teenager,' it will not be capable of being fully toilet trained. Even then, it may still make mistakes from time to time. Have faith that, if you go through the process consistently, your puppy will go through the stages of its life until it is able to exhibit the toileting behavior you require.

Chapter 2: Puppy Talk

Communication between you and your puppy is a vital aspect of toilet training. You may be discovering that the way you speak to and interact with your puppy makes a big difference. But did you know that your puppy can communicate with you about its toileting needs as well? Learning to recognize these signs and signals can make the toilet training process go a lot more smoothly.

Puppy Psychology

Puppies are in some respects creatures of habit. They respond well to regular routines. Keeping a schedule will therefore be important in toilet training. That schedule may seem inconvenient to you at first, but it will settle down into a routine that makes both you and your puppy content. In the beginning your new puppy will feel quite demanding; as the puppy grows and learns over time and you get used to your puppy's bodily rhythms, you will achieve a routine that satisfies both of the participants in the process.

Many people believe that they must train their new puppy as soon as possible, to prevent it from learning to "mark its territory." In fact, many adult dogs do not mark. Not all male dogs lift a leg to pee, and some females may learn that behavior. Whether or not your young dog is correctly socialized, or is spayed or neutered, has more to do with marking behavior than potty training.

Positive and Negative Reinforcement

"Operant conditioning" and "positive reinforcement" are behavioral theories developed by Ivan Pavlov and B.F. Skinner, respectively. You may remember learning about Pavlov's experiments with dogs, which would salivate whenever he rang a bell because they had learned to associate it with food. B.F. Skinner was a pioneer in promoting positive reinforcement, in which behaviors that are rewarded are repeated.

In terms of puppies, operant conditioning happens when a puppy associates a certain stimulus with the act of toileting, such as responding to your voice saying something like "time to go potty," as mentioned. It is a great help in toilet training.

Puppies respond very well to praise and treats. They love it when you offer them pets, kind words, and tasty rewards. These are invaluable tools in toilet training your puppy. Rather than see it as bribing your puppy, you are simply making use of positive reinforcement, one of the most powerful psychological principles in puppy toilet training.

Combining these two theories will make the whole process very effective. By sticking to a schedule, a voice command such as "time to go out" and an action—bringing the pup to the right place, you are putting operant conditioning into use. Training your puppy with positive reinforcement is a highly effective method of getting it to do what you want. Positive reinforcement means that when the puppy does what you want it to do—exhibits correct behavior—you reward it with something that the puppy really likes. This can be treats, but it can also simply be positive feedback such as praise, affection, or an activity that your puppy likes.

When your puppy responds positively by performing its toileting properly at the correct time and place, you will encourage it to repeat that good behavior if you reinforce the action with positive feedback. This is why you so often hear owners praise their puppies as "good boy" or "good girl." Some people feel that this should be done in a high-pitched, enthusiastic voice, while others feel that a quiet, soothing voice is more effective. It really doesn't matter which you choose as long as you are consistent in the way you tell your puppy that you are pleased it has learned one of its toileting lessons.

Negative reinforcement, on the other hand, means eliminating unwanted behaviors by withholding rewards or praise. In doing this, you teach the puppy that it will not receive positive feedback because it has done something contrary to its training. This means ignoring the puppy when it behaves in a way you do not want it to. That doesn't mean ignoring mistakes like wetting on the carpet. It does mean that you should simply clean up the mess without making a big deal of it. Soon enough your puppy will get the idea that it receives praise or other goodies for behaving correctly and receives nothing when it behaves incorrectly.

Negative reinforcement is often thought of as synonymous with punishment. Punishing your puppy will do no good. In fact, it may do harm. Puppies do not feel guilt, despite what you may think from their soulful gazes and lowered heads. These are actually signs of fear. Many people believe that if their puppy fears them, it will not eliminate in the wrong place. Really, though, it just means that the puppy won't want to pee or poop in front of you, so you won't have a chance to praise the puppy for doing the right thing! Remember, the puppy wants to please you, so making the puppy fearful of you is counterproductive.

Puppies can read your tone of voice and understand your body language. Of course they cower in fear when you yell at them or menace them. You would never do that to a human baby who has a lapse in its toileting behavior. You simply clean it up and move on with training. Do the same for your new puppy. It will pay dividends down the road. Your puppy will respond with love, not fear.

'Conversations' With Your Puppy

Your relationship with your puppy is a matter of give-and-take. You need to learn each other's style of communication. Your puppy will learn to tell you when it needs to go out for toileting. You'll learn to let your puppy know what your expectations are.

You may think that your puppy doesn't understand what you say. That is far from the truth. Puppies can recognize your tone of voice as positive or negative, and they are also capable of learning specific words, starting with their names.

With proper training, puppies can learn to recognize a number of words. Primary among these are the positive reinforcement words like "good dog." Later on, when they are a bit older, they can learn other commands such as 'sit' and 'stay.' For now, it's enough that they can recognize commands like "let's go for a walk" or "time to go potty." The puppy will soon associate these sounds with the behaviors you want it to accomplish.

Settle on a phrase that you will use to alert the puppy that it is time to proceed with its toileting functions and stick with it. Remember that it is the sound, not the actual words, that the pup is responding to. Changing what you say will only confuse the puppy. As in so many aspects of toilet training, consistency is key. Many people use "baby talk" with their puppies, but that's not necessary if it doesn't come naturally to you. Your tone should be friendly, open, and encouraging. An artificially high-pitched voice is not necessary, and it may even frighten your puppy at first. Your puppy will respond especially well to sincere praise when it does what you expect it to do. The same is true of when the correct behavior has been successfully accomplished. As with making connections between words and activities, choosing specific words to use for praise and using them consistently will make your meaning clear.

Your voice is not your only means of communicating with your puppy. Your facial expressions, gestures, and your use of treats or play as a means of reinforcement definitely help to get your message across to your puppy. Even eye contact can send important messages to your puppy. They know when you are glaring—it shows in your body and tone. Because dogs can use the "stare down" to communicate with each other, you want to be aware of how hard and how long you look in your dog's eyes. Puppies may be unsure at first about what is right and what is wrong; resist the urge to watch your puppy's face while it does its business. After it has finished, you can look it in the eyes with a big smile and a hearty "well done!"

Yes, your puppy can also communicate its needs to you. Puppies have their own vocabulary that you will learn to recognize as long as you remain aware and observant. Very young pups will pee almost instantly, without any signs. Week by week this changes, and patterns generally start to emerge. Puppies may bark or whine to let you know that they need to relieve themselves. They also have a number of other behaviors that can express that need. They may turn in a circle, sniff the ground, or even start to squat or, when they are older, start to lift a leg. Pay attention to these signals. They can help you determine when your puppy is ready for another lesson in toilet training.

Your Puppy's Basic Needs

You've given your puppy a home, but that's not all it needs.

Before a puppy begins toilet training, there are certain needs it has. Just like human beings, puppies cannot learn until their basic needs are met. You wouldn't expect a human child to learn if he or she didn't have a place to sleep at night or adequate, nutritious food and clean water. The same is true of puppies. If you get your puppy from a shelter, it may have been abandoned or neglected and not have the basic tools it needs for security. It's difficult if not impossible for a puppy to learn under those conditions.

What's for Dinner?

Obviously, puppies need good food. But what kind? And what kind might influence their toilet training? There's also the issue of how often you should feed your puppy.

Puppies require food specifically formulated for their dietary needs. Good puppy food will offer an easy-to-digest formula with the correct balance of vitamins, minerals, and other nutrients a growing dog needs. Whatever you feed, your puppy's food should contain minimal additives, and no added sugars and fillers. Your puppy may prefer one type of food over another, or you may discover that your puppy is allergic to certain ingredients through your trial and error process.

Be aware that dry food will expand inside the puppy's stomach, which will press against its bladder and cause a need to urinate. So will freeze-dried food. If your puppy experiences gastrointestinal upsets with symptoms such as vomiting and diarrhea, you may have to experiment with the kind of food you use.

Puppy food labels can be confusing. The content of meat in the food can be difficult to determine. There are regulations that say how much meat must be contained in a food for it to say, for example, 'chicken,' "chicken meal," "chicken flavored," or "with chicken." The American Kennel Club notes that the "*Merck Veterinary Manual* lists the recommended nutrients for dogs, along with the recommended amount by weight and age." If you have questions about what to feed, you can always refer to your puppy food dealer, your breeder, or your veterinarian.

One thing to watch is digestive upset due to feeding "people food." You may notice that dogs always want to eat some of the same foods that human beings do. Although your puppy may enjoy them, these foods are not specifically designed for puppies; they are often too rich and may contain additives or added sugars, any of which could cause gastrointestinal issues.

So, what should that feeding schedule be? A puppy should typically eat four times per day until they are three months old or so. After that, you can gradually reduce the number of feedings per day to two or three by the time your puppy is an adult dog. Leaving food out for the puppy to eat at any time of day is not a good practice. Regular feeding sessions of about 20 minutes four times a day will help regulate when your puppy will need to move its bowels and help you anticipate when your puppy will need to go out. If you got your puppy when it was quite young, less than eight to ten weeks old, it may require even more frequent feedings. But a totally weaned pup should be fine with four.

You should provide your puppy with a bowl of water at the same time that you feed it. When the water has been processed by the kidneys and bladder, the puppy will want to relieve itself—not immediately after eating and drinking, but soon thereafter.

Pay attention to your puppy's stool and urine when it does eliminate after eating. These can be important signs that your puppy may need either a change in diet or a visit to a veterinarian. Loose stool or diarrhea, constipation or straining, and blood in the urine or inability to urinate can indicate that there is something wrong with your puppy's digestive and bladder health.

Pleasing Your Puppy

As mentioned, treats to eat can be an important part of your puppy's toilet training. Like the puppy's food, they should be both tasty and nutritious. Preferably, they shouldn't contain added sugar or artificial ingredients. By trial and error, you will discover your puppy's favorite flavors, and which treats do not upset its tummy. You want to look for treats that appeal to your puppy's natural inclinations, without upsetting its delicate digestive system or causing an allergic reaction.

You will likely use treats in a number of situations, such as crate training, learning commands, and leash training. It's therefore a good idea to have one extra special goody that you reserve just for when your puppy does a good job at progressing in its toilet training. After your puppy grows into a dog and has successfully completed potty training, you can introduce more treats at various times or whenever it should receive positive reinforcement for learning another skill such as sit or stay.

Treats for your puppy can also be something other than food. Anything that your puppy enjoys will be seen as a treat and a positive reinforcement for good behavior. This can be a play session with you (not too vigorous, as this can result in the need to pee) or some time with an appropriate toy.

Examples of appropriate toys vary. A teething toy or chew toy would be a good one, as it will help the puppy learn that toys are for chewing but items such as shoes are not. A puzzle toy that a puppy can pull apart is another good choice for active pups. Toys that dispense treats are also available, but you may want to reserve those for after your puppy regularly exhibits good toileting behavior. Consider your puppy's breed and personality when you're deciding on a toy. For example, you should think about the size of your puppy as compared to the toy to prevent choking hazards. Edible chews should be removed when the size of the pieces may present a choking hazard. A new one can be used as the next reward.

Above: An appropriate, safe toy for this pug. Note that the rope toy is sized correctly for the puppy. Compare this with the plastic pot: an example of a toy that presents a choking hazard, and possible ingestion of plastic bits.

FAQ: How Does My Puppy's Personality Develop?

The age-old question regarding nature versus nurture! Personality in a puppy is determined by a number of factors. Breed, environment, amount of exercise versus confinement, and socialization will all contribute to your pup's developing personality. The use of positive over negative reinforcement is also a factor to consider.

Another thing you will notice about your puppy's personality is that it will develop over time. When a puppy is very young, it is largely helpless and dependent. A little later, as it grows into puppyhood, it will be more playful and spontaneous. It is exploring its world and will seem more mischievous as it tries to discover how things in its environment act, taste, or respond to its antics.

As the puppy grows, its personality develops along with its body. As it learns socialization skills and behaviors such as toilet training, it becomes more responsive and less flighty. This is not to say that your puppy will become completely serious. Puppies have tons of energy and love to play and be boisterous.

Perhaps the most important factor in determining your puppy's personality is your relationship with it. If you are positive and loving while still being a firm leader, your puppy will develop into a confident and well-behaved dog. If, on the other hand, you treat your puppy harshly, it is more likely to be fearful or even aggressive. Or perhaps you offer little in the way of leadership, and instead just let the puppy be a puppy, with no boundaries. Puppies need a leader; without boundaries, their explorations and behaviors can become problems that are difficult to correct.

Chapter 3: An Introduction to Toilet Training

Why is it important to do toilet training correctly? You may expect that your puppy will go outside to do its toileting business. But your puppy doesn't know that you want or expect it to do that. Although wolves and dogs in the wild live in dens that they don't like to be soiled, domesticated puppies need to be socialized to understand that.

Your Puppy's Training Needs

One reason you may choose both indoor and outdoor toilet training is if you anticipate having to leave your puppy by itself at home while you go to work. Here are some things to consider when introducing your new puppy to its new environment.

Your Puppy's New 'Den'

Because your puppy will not want to live in a soiled den, you will want to convince it that your house or apartment is its new den. You will approach this gradually by first introducing your puppy to a small space that will be its new den—it could be a crate, a playpen, or simply a confined space defined by baby gates or wire panels.

Some people tend to think of crate-training as cruel or unkind. Instead, think of the crate as a place specifically designed to discourage defecating and urinating while offering a safe, secure space just for your pup. In fact, crate training begins with the idea that the puppy will *not* use its crate for toileting.

The crate or confined space should contain a sleeping area for the puppy, as well as space for food and water dishes and a potty pad. Things to look for when considering a place for the puppy to sleep include the puppy's comfort, of course. Your puppy may prefer sleeping on a simple mat as opposed to an elaborate dog bed. And while a faux fur bed may appeal to you as being comforting because it simulates the mother's fur, it is usually quite difficult to clean. Even if the puppy doesn't use its bed as a toilet (which it might), there are other fluids such as drool or vomit to consider. A washable bed or a bed with a removable, washable outer shell is a must. It should also be very durable (puppies chew), but don't pay too much; that first bed will likely need to be replaced as your puppy grows, or the bed gets too soiled to clean. What is the right size? Most puppies prefer a bed neither too large or too small; just cozy enough to make the sleeping puppy feel more secure. Of course, some puppies can be bed hogs, and may enjoy a large soft area to sleep on.

Temperature control is important, too. Puppies seek thermal comfort, and will try to adjust according to their needs, for example, choosing a nice, cool tile floor over a dog bed on a hot day. Your puppy may prefer the cooler surface to sleep on than that fluffy, deep bed that looks perfect to you. Watch where your puppy chooses to sleep when not confined. This will clue you in to its preferences. Being able to control the temperature of the environment is key to keeping a puppy comfortable. If the puppy is kept near a doorway in winter, the area may be unusually chilly, especially at floor level, where the pup is. If the area is near windows that will allow strong sun to come in, ensure your puppy also has a shaded area to get out of that sun, in case it gets too warm. Ideally, you can choose a spot that will make sure the pup has options of both: warm and cozy, and cool and airy.

The eventual goal of toilet training is that your puppy will view your entire house or apartment as its den and refrain from soiling there. Using the crate or confined space is an essential step in this process. Coming up in this chapter, you'll learn the best way to use the crate to aid in your puppy's toilet training.

Your Puppy's External Environment

Let's take a look at other aspects of where your puppy lives, plays, and relieves itself. If your house has a yard, especially a fenced one, you may want to designate an area of it for your puppy's toileting needs. It's best to choose one area of the yard as the place for the puppy to pee and poop. After all, you don't want to encounter any waste products when you walk around in the yard, especially in summer when you or others may be in the yard barefoot.

You may want to install a low fence that the puppy will be able to jump over around the area that will be reserved for your puppy's toileting functions. This will help the puppy understand that it is to relieve itself only in that specific area.

Where will you put this outside area? There are a few different considerations. You want it to be relatively near your house because neither you nor your puppy want to have to go a long way through snow or other inclement weather. But you don't want to place it too far away at the beginning, as you want to get the pup there quickly when it begins training. Also consider that you may not want the designated toileting area to be too near a porch or deck, for example, as you, your family, and any guests may find the smell offensive.

If managed correctly, there shouldn't be that much smell. You should collect your puppy's waste at least once daily and dispose of it promptly if you want the puppy to feel comfortable using the area you select. Ideally, you will pick up any feces as soon as it happens or before the next potty time.

Cleanliness is important in getting your puppy to do its toileting in the proper place. Mistakes often happen because a puppy returns to the site where it has relieved itself in the past. They do this based on smell. If a puppy smells its own waste in a particular location, it thinks that this is an acceptable place to perform its elimination. This may not be a big problem in the great outdoors, but it certainly is inside your home!

What You Need for Puppy Training

There are several things you will need for puppy toilet training.

Since you most likely will want your puppy to ultimately toilet outdoors, you'll need an outdoor space that is convenient and large enough to let your puppy wander around a while for exercise. This can be the area of a yard that you designate or a convenient fire hydrant if you will be walking your puppy in your neighborhood.

You'll also need disposal poop bags or plain plastic bags to dispose of waste if you will be walking your puppy in public areas. A plastic scoop may be useful when cleaning up your yard, though you can also use the plastic bag over your hand to pick up the waste. Put your hand inside the plastic and pick up the stool. Then simply turn the bag inside out and seal it. It'll be neat and ready to dispose of in an appropriate receptacle.

Since your puppy requires cleanliness indoors to prevent accidents, you will need to have carpet or floor cleaning supplies on hand. Make sure that the cleaning product you choose is also a deodorizer. Puppies' sense of smell is quite keen. They will return to a place they have already used for toileting if they can smell that they have used it before. Of course, you should clean up any mistakes your puppy makes as soon as possible. Some puppy-specific cleaning products contain enzymes, natural substances that help to deep-clean any soiled spots and remove odors.

Cleaners and deodorizers are also necessary because some dogs like to "mark their territory" using urine. Their intention is to keep other dogs away, even if you don't have other dogs. It is a natural, instinctive behavior, but one that is better reserved for outside the house.

Toilet Training Supplies

In addition to cleaning supplies, there are several pieces of equipment that will make toilet training your puppy easier. Most items are readily available in pet supply shops or online.

Confined Space

A crate is the most popular confined space, which is often considered a necessity for proper puppy toilet training. It will be your puppy's own little den as you gradually get it used to its new home. There are several basic types: plastic, fabric, and wire. Each has both positives and negatives.

Plastic crates are sturdy enough that airlines permit their use in transporting animals. They consist of two shells of hard plastic, one forming the top and the other the bottom of the crate. The door is a piece of wire mesh that hooks with a secure latch. The plastic crate can make a puppy feel more secure, especially if it is spooked by noise or commotion in its vicinity. A determined puppy may be able to chew the plastic, but it shouldn't be able to get out.

Deluxe model plastic crates that are collapsible and come with a carrying handle, removable tray, divider, and wheels are available, but less expensive crates (which are still entirely serviceable) are also available in a variety of sizes.

There are also fabric 'crates' or carriers that can be used for smaller puppies, though they are generally designed only for travel/transport. These versatile carriers can even fit under the seat in front of you on an airplane or allow you to transport your puppy to the vet or to a dog park for some outdoor exercise. Such carriers aren't as sturdy as other options, though, and a puppy can rapidly outgrow them unless they are a naturally smaller breed. Dog slings, carriers, and travel bags vary from an inexpensive basic model to a pricey handmade leather tote.

Wire mesh crates allow a puppy to see and hear what is going on around it in the home. They allow for better ventilation than the plastic crate, too. Even if your puppy is one that likes seclusion and more privacy, you can simply throw a blanket over the top of the wire crate for quiet times.

Above: A good size crate for this young pup. Note the mat and toys.

While a variety of crates are available and relatively inexpensive, they don't really provide enough room to have the entire area dedicated for a puppy, especially for a growing puppy. Larger wire crates and kennels sell at price ranges from low to moderate. an option either instead of a crate or combined with one is a portable exercise pen. These provide your puppy more room to play and are an affordable option, and are often available in coated wire or plastic, making moving and cleaning easier. Putting a crate inside the play area, or just using a bed in the space can both work.

Whatever kind of confined space you choose, it should be large enough for your puppy to stand or sit, lie down, and turn around. If there is more room than that in the crate or playpen, it should contain a bed or sleeping mat at one end and a toileting area at the other. If you must leave your puppy alone for long periods, this may be the best solution.

The crate or kennel should also be easily moveable in order to locate it in an area where the puppy feels most comfortable. For instance, if you live in a cold climate or have air conditioning, the puppies may prefer a warmer location. You will want to be able to move the crate to a room that has more foot traffic during the day so the puppy can become socialized to the people in your household during the day, and perhaps to your bedroom at night so you can easily take the puppy to its toileting area for a nighttime outing. Especially at the beginning, the primary need is for the puppy to feel safe. This means the puppy must be able to feel, hear, see, and smell the presence of the 'pack.' A location that is somewhat central and busy is therefore best.

Should you get a crate based on the size that your puppy is now or based on the size it will be when it grows into an adult dog? Wire cages sometimes come with movable panels that can be used to partition off part of the crate while the puppy is small and then moved or removed as the puppy grows. Overly large crates may tempt the puppy to use a portion of the space for toileting; too small and it won't be able to move around comfortably. Of course, you can also buy a smaller crate at first, and upgrade to a larger one as your puppy grows up. Often you can find a used crate or playpen at a yard sale or from a neighbor who no longer needs theirs. (You can donate the old crate to a rescue shelter—they will be glad to have it.)

As mentioned before, the space for your puppy does not need to include a crate, and many people prefer this. You can confine your puppy to an enclosed, easily cleanable area of the house, preferably with no carpeting. In fact, if possible, remove any area rugs; once soiled, the odor may remain and confuse your puppy, as well as ruin your rug! If not possible consider getting a remnant of vinyl flooring to put over the carpet for the time being.

A gate in a doorway can keep the puppy in a specific room and will prevent the puppy from entering areas of the house where you don't want the pup to be or are unable to monitor behavior. And puppy gates are an affordable option. One drawback to this method is that unless the room is near the center of the action in the house, your puppy may feel isolated and lonely. This can lead to a poorly socialized pup, or one that learns to bark or whine for attention. A playpen type of arrangement can be a great compromise, allowing your puppy the security of the enclosed space with the ability to see everything that is going on. Another plus is the ability to move the playpen to different locations, depending on where the family tends to be at given times throughout the day.

Potty Pads

You can purchase disposable pads that your puppy can use when you have to be out of the house for much of the day. Some pads are even made of artificial grass so they simulate an outdoor environment. There are even reusable potty pads. Whatever kind of pad you choose, try to place it in an area away from both where you feed and water the puppy and its sleeping area. Like the place where a puppy sleeps, the area where it eats is not a place where it will want to relieve itself.

Of course, you don't have to use potty pads at all, though they can be useful in early toilet training or if you live in an apartment where there are stairs or an elevator and a lobby that makes it difficult to get a young puppy outdoors in time to meet its toileting needs. This is especially important when it is first learning proper toileting etiquette. You can use potty pads all the time if you desire and are willing to pay for them Or you can use them only when the weather is bad and you aren't able to take your puppy outdoors.

A quick check on the internet will provide you with many sources of potty pads, which can range in cost. If you plan to rely primarily on indoor training, it is most cost effective to buy in bulk, or to set up a regularly scheduled reorder shipping plan. Trays are available to help hold the pad in place and to make clean-up easier. An alternative to potty pads is a flat tray-like container filled with dog litter. You can also train your puppy to use litter pellets—with or without odor control—similarly to the way you house train a kitten. Litter trays for both large and small breeds are also available. Check for these items online, or they may also be available for pick up at your local pet store.

Some puppies may use their potty pads as a bed. This could be because the sleeping surface is not comfortable for them for some reason—generally too warm—or simply a choice. If they use the pad for pottying, and use it to sleep on, too, you'll want to dissuade this. Try to figure out why the puppy prefers the pad for sleeping, and adjust its sleeping area accordingly. You can also place objects on the pad itself, such as a brick or stones, to allow enough space to comfortably relieve themselves but not enough for sleeping on. Placing stones on the potty pad will also help keep it in the place you desire, and make it more difficult for the puppy to drag it around as a toy.

If your puppy seems distressed that its bed is gone, you can always leave it one pad for pottying and one for sleeping. Leave them a distance apart, and always in the same location. Using an attractant—either a bit of the puppy's urine or commercially available drops or a spray—will help the puppy know which pad is for what purpose.

Just as you will do for the confined area in general, keep the potty pads clean. Most dogs will use a potty pad three to five times at most before it is deemed too dirty, and many will not use a pad again for any purpose once there is feces on it.

Collar, Leash, or Harness

A collar or a harness and a leash will be necessary, at least at first, if you want to take your puppy outside for walks and toileting, even if only going to your yard. You can get your puppy used to having a collar or harness on gradually, putting it on for just a few minutes when you first start training your puppy. If your puppy whines or tugs at the collar, don't worry. Simply start slowly—perhaps five minutes wearing the collar—and increase the amount of time as the puppy grows used to it.

There are many styles and types of collars available. What kind of collar should you choose? It should be adjustable in size so that you can expand it as your puppy grows. People often believe that it will be less distressing to your puppy if you put the collar on loosely, but this is a mistake. A collar that is too loose can let your puppy get the collar into its jaws and get caught, or the collar may get caught on other objects, either scenario creating a choking hazard. And slipping out of a loose collar is quite easy for a squirming, active puppy. A good rule of thumb is that the collar, when properly placed high up on the neck just behind the ears, should allow you to slip two fingers in, but no more. Puppies grow very quickly so it is a good idea to check the fit and adjust accordingly every few days.

The most popular choice is a collar made of sturdy but flexible nylon straps. The same is true for leashes. Harnesses also come in different sizes, materials, and configurations. It is probably not worth spending a lot on your puppy's first collar, as it may outgrow even an adjustable collar. The best bet is to get something that fits your puppy well now, and for the near future; in other words, don't try to get a collar for your nine week old Rottweiler puppy that will fit them when they are fully grown!

When to use a harness, collar, or halter comes down to what the objective is. In most cases people don't want a dog to pull. In some cases they do. For certain types of working dogs this choice is more suitable than that. In certain cases, safety is more of a concern than usual due to the dog's nature and state of mind. So equipment should be chosen specifically for the purpose or goal.

Unless there is something very specific or unusual about the pup, you can buy both a harness and collar to start with. This is more for convenience than anything else, allowing you to experiment and find what works best for you and your puppy. Having your puppy on just a collar means less material, therefore less potential for chafing. It also allows the feel of more freedom and it's easier to train nice leash walking. For toilet training purposes some people may prefer a harness, especially very young pups. A good fit and soft material is key. Find one with both front and back rings; this offers more options when leash training.

Puppies that will become working dogs may dictate what choice you make; some dogs will eventually be asked to pull, so a harness is a good option. Some will need to guide, and some will only be expected to be a good companion. Whether collar or leash, it all comes down to your preference and needs, and what seems to work best for your pup.

For toilet training, tools such as a full choke chain, prong collar, or e-collar should be avoided. They are not only inappropriate for the job, they are unnecessary, and can potentially create behavioral issues. There are much better and kinder ways.

Above: A well-fitted collar and harness. Note that leather and other expensive choices may not be the best at first, as your puppy will likely outgrow them.

Sprays as a Reinforcement

Another training aid that you may want to get is an area spray. Sprays can be found in three varieties. There are sprays that will steer your puppy away from areas where you do not want it to pee or poop (repellents), and sprays that help encourage it that this is the right place to go (attractants). These are different from the kind of spray that you use to clean up puppy messes so the puppy won't return to where it has made mistakes before. Cleaning products work to neutralize and therefore deodorize the scent of a previous incident. Attractant sprays contain pheromones blended to encourage your puppy to go in that area. Repellents have a smell that is unpleasant to the puppy; it will avoid that area generally for any purpose, so keep it away from eating and sleeping areas. These products can generally be used both indoors and out, with attractants to encourage use of the potty pad or a particular area of the yard, and repellents to protect areas you do not want it to soil, such as an expensive rug, your sofa, or a flower bed.

Although they can be helpful, sprays alone are usually not enough. Puppies still need training to make the connections. Just because you sprayed an attractant in one area of your lawn does not mean your puppy will learn to only go there, or it may not even find the right spot without guidance if there are other interesting odors around.

Repellent sprays will not harm or frighten the puppy. The amount needed is generally very small, and the scent can range from strong to almost undetectable. Using a combination of both natural and synthetic attractants, plus inert ingredients like water or oils, they are not considered harmful to your puppy when used according to the directions.

Identification

There's always the chance that your puppy will get away from you when you take it outdoors. Therefore, it's a good idea for your puppy to have a means of identification. You can get your puppy an ID tag with your address and phone that will hang from its collar, right along with its vaccination tag. But if your puppy manages to get out of its collar, the ID is gone too.

It makes sense to have your puppy microchipped. This is a harmless procedure that can be accomplished in a veterinarian's office. A small chip is placed under the puppy's skin at the base of the neck or between the shoulderblades. It links to a special number and is easily readable using a special receiver. You register your puppy's chip with a service that stores the chip's contents and is cross-referenced to your information. If someone finds your wayward pup, it will be easy to take it to the vet, read the chip, and get your puppy back to you.

FAQ: Isn't Toilet Training a Puppy Difficult?

It depends on what is meant by 'difficult.' The process can be frustrating, or feel like it is taking forever. It may seem like an imposition on your time to properly monitor your pup. Remember, you invited the puppy to your house, so you must create the setting that will help your puppy become a happy addition to the household. If you approach toilet training your puppy at the right age and in a consistent manner with friendly, encouraging communication, you will find it much easier to achieve success.

Some breeds of dogs have the reputation of being difficult to toilet train. Small breeds, for example, have smaller bladders and so aren't able to "hold it" for as long. The "scent hounds" such as bassets and beagles may have difficulty overcoming their mistakes because they will be attracted to the odor of a spot where they have previously soiled more so than other puppies. Regardless, done properly, all breeds and sizes can be potty trained.

There isn't just one method of toilet training your puppy. A combination of several methods may work best. You can experiment with various types of training that will meet both your puppy's needs and your own. Next we'll examine the basic steps of toilet training.

Chapter 4: The Process of Toilet Training

So now you've brought your new puppy home and stocked up on the supplies you'll need. How does toilet training actually happen? What do you need to do?

You may want to begin your puppy's toilet training on a Friday so you will have the whole weekend together and can make early progress. If you can spend longer at home with your puppy, that's great! You can get a lot of lessons in over a few days, though remember, completely training a puppy can't be accomplished in that short a time.

You should try to have an alternate, trusted caregiver or family member available to care for the puppy when you cannot. You may also need to be away in the future and will want to be able to have another person such as a pet sitter or dog-walker care for your puppy at those times.

Remember that you and your puppy are in this together. You want your puppy to behave properly and your puppy wants to please you. By approaching toilet training with a proper attitude and a willingness to take it gradually, you and your puppy can both get what you need. Just remember: patience and practice are the keys!

The Beginning: Using the Crate

The crate or other confined space is the most valuable tool you have when it comes to toilet training a puppy. A properly sized and furnished crate will serve as your puppy's security spot, and should not be used as a place of isolation and punishment. As a general rule of thumb, the size of the confined space should be approximately three times the puppy's length and one and a half times its width, certainly no smaller.

The crate should contain a towel, mat, blanket, or even a piece of your old clothing for the puppy to sleep on. Using a piece of clothing will help the puppy get used to your scent which can encourage it to come to you as a place where it can feel warmth, security, and love. You can even put a small dog bed in the confined space if you and your puppy want that.

Some crates contain dishes attached to the side that provide your puppy with a place for food or water. Confined puppy spaces can also contain elevated food and water dishes in little pans that reduce mess from spills. This may help if you must leave the puppy in the crate for long periods of time, though ultimately you will want to have the puppy eat in a convenient place in the home such as the kitchen. If you can offer your puppy regular frequent access to clean water, this may be preferable to leaving water in the crate.

Some puppy toys are also useful additions to the confined space. They will provide something for your puppy to play with, chew, and be distracted by. If you have used playtime with toys as a way to reward a puppy for learning the process of toilet training, it will look upon the toys as a form of 'treat.' It bears repeating that the crate or confined space should not be used as a place of punishment or isolation; it should become a portion of the home that belongs to the puppy.

Depending on your puppy's personality, you may want to place the crate in different areas. If your puppy seems nervous or overexcitable, try a quiet space where the puppy won't be distracted by sights, sounds, and motion. If your puppy is outgoing and interested in activities around it, you might put the crate in a common area such as the living room or kitchen. And you may want to take the puppy's crate into your bedroom at night, since you will likely be getting up to take the puppy out to relieve itself.

Introduce Your Puppy to the Confined Space

When you bring your new puppy home, you will want to introduce it to its new home-within-a-home. Place the crate in the confined living area where you expect your puppy to be most comfortable. Leave the door to the crate open. The crate, along with the playpen or gated area, will be just another aspect of the environment that the puppy will want to explore.

Bit by bit, help your puppy get used to going into the confined space. Give it positive reinforcement when it does so on its own. You can help the puppy learn that the space is a good place to be by placing a favorite treat inside. Your pup will need to "follow its nose" into the crate to get the treat. This will instantly reward the puppy for going in and exploring its new den, as will praise. At this point, you may be tempted to close the door or gate and 'trap' the puppy, but resist! Allow your new friend to wander in and out for now. Before long, it will become just another part of the home environment.

Encourage your puppy to spend more time in the confined space. You can start closing the crate door or baby gate for a brief time—maybe 30 seconds or so—while your puppy is inside. If you see your puppy go into the confined space on its own, give it praise—a play session, treat, or a verbal expression of satisfaction. It's a good sign if the puppy does go into the space by itself. It means that the puppy is becoming comfortable with the crate or other den area, a reaction that will pay off during toilet training.

Gradually increase the time your puppy spends in the crate, from a few seconds to a minute to three to five minutes to ten or fifteen and then to half an hour. Eventually you will want the puppy to be able to spend several hours comfortably in its special area and hold its pee and poop while you are away from the house for work or for other reasons. It's too much to expect a puppy to do at first, but if that is one of your goals, now is the time to start.

If the puppy seems upset about being in the confined space, limit sessions to short periods. You don't want your new puppy to get the idea that being confined is a punishment. Even if the puppy has an accident and soils elsewhere in the house, don't put it in the crate for being 'bad.' At this point in toilet training, the puppy will not realize that it has done anything wrong. Until the puppy has gotten farther along in its toilet training, its natural instinct is to relieve itself wherever it is when it feels the need to do so.

If the puppy stays in the crate for more than two to three hours, whether for a nap or other reason, take the puppy outdoors or to its potty pad to toilet as soon as you let it out of the confined space. Although the puppy will probably try to avoid soiling in its new den, it's best to reinforce this by letting it have the opportunity to relieve itself when it does come out.

Establish a Schedule

Puppies learn by repetition. Like human beings, they respond well to established routines. These condition the puppy's body and mind to respond to toilet training appropriately and continue with their good toileting habits even after they no longer need constant attention and reinforcement.

You will need to take your puppy outside—or to the indoor potty pad—to begin its official toilet training. Let the puppy become used to the area where you want it to relieve itself, but don't let it wander too freely. You can definitely use the collar and leash to guide and keep the puppy to the area you have selected. Don't drag the puppy there, of course, but use the leash to gently let your puppy know this is where you want it to be.

A schedule is particularly important if you are only trying to do outdoor training. It's true that you may have to do this as many as twelve times a day to begin with (about every hour or two), which is why starting on a weekend is recommended. You'll want to take your puppy out first thing in the morning, of course. Whenever the puppy eats and drinks, wait about 20 minutes before you go out. This will give the food and water some time to work their way through the puppy's system, but not so long that they can't hold it. Remember that at first you will be feeding your puppy up to four times a day. You'll be reducing the number of feedings gradually over the coming days: from four times a day until they are at least three months old to a minimum of two times per day when the puppy is fully grown. As your puppy grows and has fewer feedings, it will also be gaining better control over its bowels, so these potty breaks will become fewer and farther between.

After playtime is another occasion when you want to schedule visits to the toileting area. Playtime makes puppies excited. Sometimes that makes them unable to hold their urine. You may be able to schedule playtime out of doors, or just take the puppy out after a vigorous play session. Chewing in particular activates a puppy's need to eliminate, so if the play involves chew toys, be extra sure to schedule a toilet break afterward.

Puppies also feel the need to perform their toileting functions after taking a nap, just like first thing in the morning, so pay attention to your puppy's sleeping habits—and your own. It is useful to stress that first thing in the morning is an occasion when you should definitely see to the puppy's toileting needs as soon as possible.

You will of course want to take the puppy out to relieve itself just before you turn in for the night. While your puppy is young, you should also accept the fact that it will want to go out during the night as well. Set an alarm clock so that you will wake up in about three to four hours, which should be around the time that the puppy needs to go out. As the puppy gets older, you will be able to eliminate this middle-of-the-night outing.

Understand Your Puppy's Signals

You may be able to determine from your puppy's 'tells' or signals when it needs to go out for a toilet session. When they are about to relieve themselves, puppies often sniff or turn in a circle. They may squat if they are about to urinate (or lift a leg as male puppies get older), or walk with a hunched appearance if they are about to defecate.

If your puppy performs one of these behaviors, immediately scoop it up and carry it to its designated toileting area. When you catch your puppy before it soils in an unapproved place and then take it to where you have designated as the place to relieve itself, you will be reinforcing the idea that one place is a no-no and the other is good. Naturally, praise the puppy after it does its toileting where you want it to. If your puppy tries to get to the right area, and is close, particularly with a potty pad, it is okay to gently move the puppy over a bit. Just try not to disturb its business. Give your puppy some privacy by remaining a quiet presence while it does its necessaries. Praise and party afterwards; getting excited while your puppy is busy may distract it, and prevent an important lesson from being learned. And don't stare, as dogs may interpret steady eye contact as discomfiting, so just keep a casual eye on the action.

When your puppy is very young, you will likely need to pick it up each time—gently, with a hand supporting its bottom—and carry it to the right location, either outside or on the grass mat or potty pad. If you can't get the puppy to the toileting spot, simply clean up the mess and let the incident go. You can't expect a young puppy to get the idea right away. Good bowel and bladder control will come later.

Your Puppy's Progress

Your puppy is home, and you've loaded up on supplies. Now what?

For the first few days up to a few weeks, there will be accidents. Lots of them, most likely. You'll clean them up as has been discussed: no fuss, or punishment, just clean and deodorize. Your puppy may be young enough that you will have to carry them to the designated potty area(s). Once there, let them move freely about while keeping them in the correct area. Whenever your puppy goes where you want it to, it's time to throw that party! Don't scare you pup, just give lots of happy praise, pets, and a special treat or two.

When you and your puppy are finished, move away from the area. This will give you an opportunity to clean up, if necessary, and will begin to teach your puppy that the area is for one purpose only. Should your puppy go in an area you have not designated for toileting, but it is close, praise them modestly. Reserve all praise if your puppy goes someplace you regard as out of bounds. Remember to be neutral, not angry.

You can help your puppy identify good areas to go with a few tricks. Bringing it to the same area of the yard where it has gone before will certainly help. The same for an area where another dog has gone. For the puppy this won't be marking per se, it will just be clear that others have gone there before.

Another idea is to put a bit of your puppy's own urine on a potty pad, perhaps from an accident. Then leave that pad in the area for the pup to use. It will learn to go where it knows it has already gone. You only need a tiny bit; don't leave a soiled pad in with your puppy, as it may find it distasteful. A pup's sense of smell is far superior to ours, even at that young age. If you can smell it, it is probably too much.

Setting a Schedule for Outdoor Training

If you plan on only training your puppy to do its business outside, the schedule you set at the beginning may look something like this:

- Early in the morning, pick up the puppy and bring it outside. Don't waste time with collars and leashes, or coaxing to the door. Your puppy needs to go! Just get it where you want that to happen. It may only urinate at this time; that's totally fine.

- In a little while it will be time for breakfast. Set this for a time that works for you, perhaps after a shower or the first cup of coffee. Keep it on the early side, as you will be needing to fit in three to four meals each day for a little while.

- After waiting 15-20 minutes, or until you think you see signs from your pup (sniffing, circling, preparing to squat), take them back out for a walk or some play time in the yard near the preferred toileting area. Your puppy will likely have a bowel movement fairly quickly. Like people, all pups are different and some may need more time to have the urge, some less. Try to be patient. If your pup doesn't go within 20-30 minutes, you can go back inside for an hour, then try again.

- Mid-morning, lunchtime, midafternoon, suppertime, you will repeat the process. You can just go on the schedule, or if you can watch the puppy, look for those signs as the time approaches. You will fit in the extra meal or two around those times, but do not give the pup any more food after the dinner meal and walk.

The reason that your puppy will absolutely need an outing in the middle of the night is because young puppies are unable to hold on for more than a few hours. Even if they are old enough to be capable of waiting, they need to be taught to do so. They need to learn to hold it physically, and also have faith they will be allowed to go out when they need to.

Fortunately, this outing, like the extra meals, will be unnecessary as your pup develops. Somewhere between twelve to fifteen weeks is a good benchmark to use for getting down to two meals a day and only a late night and early morning excursion. You can help your puppy adjust to longer sleep and quiet time at night by making the evening outing later and the morning one earlier until your pup seems comfortable waiting. Signs of progress include no accidents, and finding a relatively calm pup first thing in the morning.

Setting a Schedule for Indoor Training

The schedule for indoor training will be very similar. Timing is important. If your puppy is confined to a crate or small space with no pottying area, you will need to bring the pup to a toileting area as often as you would bring it outside. If the space is large enough to include a toileting area, giving hints like the pre-treated potty pad (there are some products available if you find using a bit of your puppy's pee distasteful), or a low barrier that defines the right corner to use are helpful.

When letting your puppy have free time in its designated space outside the crate, try to remain alert in case your puppy does its business exactly where you want it, so you can give praise and treats to reinforce that activity as a good one.

You can absolutely teach your puppy to use a designated area both indoors and in the great outdoors! This can be a big plus if you need to be away for several hours during the day from time to time, or if quick access to the outdoors is not possible. The concern here is that the pup may confuse the idea that since going anywhere outside is good, therefore going anywhere inside is also good. Yet another reason to train your puppy to consistently use the preferred toileting area.

Above: A perfect puppy! Next up, treats, praise and a party to help instill this as a desired behavior.

Techniques for Success

It cannot be overstated that remembering and using a few key points can mean the difference between steady success versus inconsistent toileting behavior. Timing and scheduling are paramount. If you maintain a consistent schedule for mealtimes, and adhere to an equally regular schedule for outings—adjusted as you learn more about your individual puppy's abilities and preferences—you will achieve a reliable amount of success in a shorter time. Yes, accidents will still happen, but by being consistent you help your puppy learn to adjust its behaviors and needs more easily than with random feedings and trips to the appropriate toileting area.

Another 'pro-tip' for learning about your puppy in order to establish an optimal schedule and avoid accidents is to bring your puppy to the desired area and remain there while your pup does its business. Avoid simply putting the puppy out in the yard, or in the area with the potty pad. You want the information you will get from watching how long it takes for the pup to urinate, and exactly where it chooses to go. You'll also learn how frequently your puppy needs to defecate; just as some adult dogs poop only once a day, and others twice (hopefully not more), your puppy will develop its own habits. If you don't know that your puppy took a long pee, or did not accomplish a bowel movement during a particular outing, you will be guessing as to what was done. Putting a puppy that has not had a morning poop into an enclosed area for several hours will—in all likelihood—guarantee an accident occurs.

As you have discovered, although there are some definite do's and don'ts when toilet training, there is no one correct way to toilet train your new puppy. What follows are several different scenarios that enjoyed great success for both the puppies and the owners. By reviewing these examples, you should get some good ideas to use for your own training program.

The Perfect Set-Up #1: Dale and Stephen and Buster

Dale and John brought Buster home on a Friday morning. They had the day off, and Monday was a holiday, giving them four full days of nothing but puppy time. They had set up a designated area in the main entryway; the open floorplan meant that Buster would be able to see almost all of the household activity: at the front door, inside the living and dining rooms, and even through a large doorway into the kitchen. The floor there was tile—an impervious, easy-to-clean surface. The area was defined by a set of panels that could be added to as Buster grew (think playpen with no floor). It was light enough to move if wanted, but its central location meant that might not be necessary.

Inside the space was a crate with a sleeping pad, the door to which was left open. In one corner of the space was an absorbent mat with a heavy-based water bowl. This was also where the feed dish would go when it was meal time. In the corner farthest from the crate was a potty pad and a fake grass potty mat; they wanted their new family member to be able to choose.

Another enclosed area—this one much smaller—was by the bed. This would keep it cozy for the pup and also create easy access for Dale and Stephen when it was time for a middle of the night trip outside. Being this close also allowed for them all to bond more quickly. This space was just big enough for a sleeping area with a choice of a warm mat or cool floor. The floor was actually a piece of vinyl flooring placed over the carpet, just in case of an accident, without providing an explicit place for the puppy to go.

Buster hardly used the crate but loved the beds. As the pup grew, they got rid of the crate, and expanded the designated area by adding more panels. Buster was also allowed time to be free in the house with the couple—under supervision. They wanted to trust the puppy, and for the puppy to trust them. Puppies and dogs are pack animals in that they prefer socialization and being a part of a group. Buster was kept in on all the comings and goings, and was never isolated from Dale or Stephen. This set-up, in turn, gave Buster's owners a very good chance of witnessing pre-pottying behavior and also to be aware of what was happening and when. The puppy was praised heartily for good deeds, ignored for mistakes, and given treats to reinforce positive behaviors. Later on, these habits of praise and reward that were instilled from the start would become a big help for further command training. All in all, it was an ideal set-up that worked perfectly for this puppy and its people.

The Perfect Set-Up #2: Danny and Doobie

Doobie was already partially crate-trained when Danny brought the puppy home. There was a small crate from a previous dog which would work until Doobie outgrew it. Danny only wanted Doobie to do business outside, so they were prepared for many trips to the yard during the first few weeks. One corner of the yard was chosen for pooping; Doobie was allowed to pee almost anywhere in the yard—under supervision, of course. After business was done, Doobie would get a long walk or a solid play session before going back to the crate.

Because Danny worked at home most of the time, this was a relatively easy accommodation to make. Their work did sometimes require them to be in the office all day. Knowing that, Danny located a midday dogwalker right away. The dogwalker was asked to come by for a visit several times while Danny was home and to bring their own dog. This would allow Doobie to have some socialization with both different people and other dogs.

When it was time to be working, Doobie was in the crate by Danny's desk during nap time, and allowed to wander in a small space between the desk and the bookcase while awake. A variety of toys were available for Doobie to play with. At night, when the pup was still small, Danny would move the crate to the bedroom and settle Doobie in, then set an alarm for a 2:00 a.m. walk in the yard.

By the time Doobie was just over 12 weeks old, the pup could wait up to four hours before needing a break outside. The dog walker would come by about three hours after Danny left for the office, take Doobie to yard to go, then take both dogs for a walk for up to an hour. The dogwalker knew how to be patient with a new puppy on the leash; the presence of their own dog behaving well on walks helped Doobie learn quickly. Danny arranged a schedule to be able to return home about three hours after that outing. The routine seemed to work well for everyone.

As the puppy grew, Danny stopped using the crate by getting Doobie used to dog beds in different areas. The crate was not removed "cold turkey," but rather the puppy was allowed to discover for itself that the crate was too small, and the bed safe and comfortable.

The Perfect Set-Up #3: Kate and Leah and Matcha

Perhaps you are more like Kate and Leah, who did not want their puppy in the bedroom at night. In order to accomplish this and prevent the puppy from feeling isolated, they came up with a few ways to keep Matcha content all night.

Matcha's designated space was similar to Buster's. It was an area near the back door fenced by two dog gates, with a water bowl, a roomy crate, sleeping mat and potty pad. Their goal was to have their puppy go outside, but they wanted Matcha to learn what the potty pad was for, in case they had to leave the puppy alone inside for a while. In the earliest stages of training, they would watch for signs and bring Matcha to the potty pad instead of outside. They had already pre-marked the pad with a tiny bit of the puppy's own scent.

Because a bored or lonely puppy can be a destructive puppy, Kate and Leah always made sure there was a long-lasting treat or favorite toy in the area to keep Matcha busy. The gentle activity also helped settle the puppy down for quiet time.

At night, after the last walk, Matcha would be given a treat to go into the crate. Inside there was a simple mat, a favorite toy, and one of Leah's old sweatshirts. Having an article of clothing with an owner's scent on it allows the puppy to feel as if the person is there, offering a sense of security. In order to keep the puppy feeling less isolated during the night, they set up a way to play an audiobook at low volume so it would feel as if there was someone speaking all the time. Talk radio stations worked, too.

When Matcha was able to hold her pottying for about five hours, they let her have the whole designated area overnight, leaving the door of the crate open so the pup could choose where to be.

FAQ: How Long Will My Puppy Be Able to "Hold It" While I'm Away at Work?

At first, not long at all. That's why it's best to have another family member or alternate caregiver available to take over caring for the puppy's toileting needs when it's starting its training if you cannot attend to it yourself. But take heart! A puppy's ability to hold its waste increases as the puppy gets older. In general, a puppy will be able to refrain from soiling for the number of hours that corresponds to the age of the puppy in months. Therefore, a puppy of two months will be able to hold its urine and feces for a total of two hours. The limit to this is when the puppy reaches nine months old. After all, you probably aren't able to "hold it" for ten or more hours, either!

Think about it. Puppy physiology is similar to human physiology. We all take in food and liquids. These go through the stomach and into the bowels and kidneys, then through the colon and the bladder, then into the outside world. Human beings have to be trained to hold their waste products when they are babies, and the process isn't complete for several years. Until then, the infant soils its diaper whenever and wherever it is. The same is true for puppies. They experience the same bodily processes and must go through similar training, although fortunately for a puppy owner, it is a much shorter time.

Chapter 5: What Works and What Doesn't

Some tactics work well when you are toilet training a puppy—others not so much. What makes some techniques successful and others doomed to failure? Primary among the least successful are ones that don't follow the basic principles of training your puppy: rewards and praise, consistency, and a positive attitude.

Clicker Training

As an alternative to the positive reinforcement and crate training already described, you may have success with clicker training. Clickers are small, inexpensive handheld devices, often made of plastic, that produce a clicking noise when squeezed. Although a clicker can be used for either positive or negative reinforcement, positive is always better, and falls in line with the ethos of this training program. It can be used for a number of training applications and scenarios other than toilet training, making it a useful and productive training tool.

By praising the dog for a wanted behavior and also clicking the clicker, followed by a reward, you can eventually teach the pup that the clicker means the same as "good dog!" After a while you can drop the verbal command, and keep the clicker and reward. Occasionally delay giving the treat, or omit it all together, to allow the puppy to learn that the clicker noise is a positive response from you. In a sense, this can create an ability for "delayed gratification." The click is first associated with praise and a reward immediately. After a period of time, the click will come to mean the same thing by itself. A treat will be an added bonus.

However, a clicker always sounds the same and does not allow the variation of a human voice and body language. At times, this may have benefits and be preferred. The click is a consistent, reliable sound, and can be used easily. Advantages to using your voice, however, are many. By using your voice with changing tones and hand signals, you can provide more detailed feedback to the dog. There are levels of "yes, you're on the right track," and levels of "no, please try again" that can be conveyed through voice and tone.

Although a clicker is less personal and does not allow for subtlety, it can be helpful as a harmless kind of negative reinforcement. Note that though a clicker may be used for *either* positive or negative feedback, it cannot be used for *both* positive and negative feedback. As with all commands, consistency is key.

When you want your puppy to understand that a place or thing is off limits, tell the puppy 'no' and click the clicker. Then remove the stimulus that is off limits to the puppy, or move the puppy. For example, move a plant to a higher shelf or guide the puppy away from an area where it is not supposed to relieve itself, such as a flower bed. A gentle tug on the puppy's leash will reinforce the command and the clicking sound.

By giving a treat when it displays the behavior you want it to, the puppy will associate the sound of the clicker with the command of 'no' and the attempted action. Eventually, the puppy will respond to the sound of the clicker without you having to give the command verbally.

Using the clicker in this way is a measure you can take when the puppy is first learning the difference between things that are permitted and things that aren't. You may want to take the clicker with you when you go for walks at first. Gradually the puppy will come to learn that the place or object is forbidden without hearing the sound of the clicker.

Punishment and Scolding

It's difficult not to be annoyed with your puppy when it has accidents or appears to have forgotten what it has learned so far about proper toileting etiquette. Even though you have this feeling, it's not a good idea to show it to your puppy. This will be counterproductive and may actually set back its toilet training. Remember how valuable positive reinforcement is and how poorly negative reinforcement works.

Punishing your puppy is the wrong approach. Harsh words will undo all the progress you and the puppy have made through praise and rewards. Your puppy does want to please you. You should praise the puppy when it performs the way you want it to and ignore it when the puppy makes a mistake.

If you catch your puppy in the act of soiling, you can respond by telling your puppy 'no' using a firm voice, but don't yell or speak harshly. Your puppy may not understand your words, but it can certainly tell by your tone of voice and even your body language that your words communicate displeasure. Use your voice to express disappointment, and be firm but gentle in tone. There is no need to speak at high volume to a puppy; keep the level down to a three out of ten.

And definitely don't act out your anger physically. The puppy simply won't understand. Just clean up the mess without a lot of fuss. Be sure to use a deodorizer so that the puppy won't think it has found a good place to eliminate.

If you notice your puppy's signals that it is about to relieve itself, the best thing you can do is to scoop up the pup immediately and rush to where it is supposed to pee and poop. Then tell the puppy something encouraging like "good boy!" or "that's right."

If you must return the puppy to its crate after an accident (try to avoid this), do so in a positive way, not by carrying anger from the accident. The crate is supposed to be a comfortable den, not a place of punishment. You want your puppy to like being in the cozy crate, not fear and hate it. The crate is an important training tool that will only work if the puppy tolerates being in it for increasingly longer periods of time. And that can't happen if the crate is used in a negative way.

Overuse of Crate Training

That said, don't rely on the puppy's crate as the only training tool. Collar and leash time are important too, especially to get your puppy used to the idea of relieving itself out of doors. Making your puppy stay in the crate for more time than it has become comfortable with may lead to other unwanted behaviors such as barking or whining. If you can't be home, make sure that there is a responsible person around to let the puppy out at regular intervals.

You also don't want to have the puppy spend too much time in the crate because you want to instill other qualities in your puppy. You want it to learn how to play nicely with both human beings and any other pets. That includes all of the other members of your household, as well as strangers you may encounter. In particular, a child needs to learn how to interact with the puppy, as well as the puppy needing to learn to behave appropriately with the child. Having all members of the household participate, even in a small way, in toilet training can instill good relationships all around. Collar and leash training can also be very useful when you want to teach your puppy other commands such as 'sit' and 'stay,' which cannot be learned inside the crate.

Perhaps most important of all, remember that dogs are social animals. Puppies in particular want to be in on the action. They are a member of your family, too, so don't keep them locked away, alone, until it is convenient for you to deal with them.

Myths About Puppy Toilet Training
Puppies Must Be Six Months Old Before Toilet Training Begins

This is not only untrue, it's counterproductive. Puppies can and should begin toilet training as early as eight to ten weeks old, and will have made significant progress by the time they are five months old. They can become used to staying in their confined space for longer and longer periods of time and to hold their eliminations while in their substitute den.

This misconception may stem from advice on what age a puppy should be before it is neutered. Puppies that are neutered too late can pick up bad habits such as spraying to mark their territory, even inside the house. Consult with your veterinarian for advice on when you should have your puppy spayed or neutered.

Puppies can learn a lot of toilet training principles when they are younger than six months. Of course, a puppy doesn't have the muscular control to hold its waste when it is newborn and must acquire the skill gradually. But if you wait too long, the puppy may acquire bad habits that are hard to break. Puppies can begin to be habituated to toileting areas as early as two to three months old, which is when they are ready to come home with you anyway.

You Can't Teach an Old Dog New Tricks

Conversely, many people believe that toilet training cannot start when a puppy is older. That may be why they are reluctant to adopt full-grown dogs from a shelter. While it may seem more difficult due to negative behaviors the dog may have developed, never fear! Toilet training can be taught or re-learned at any age, regardless if the dog is older and has forgotten its training.

We're focusing on puppies, rather than older dogs, but for now just know that it's entirely possible. You can still bring an older dog into its "forever home" and have confidence that it can learn to behave properly.

My Puppy Hasn't Learned Because It Is Stubborn or Stupid

Above: Is this a naughty puppy?

If your puppy has not learned how, where, and when to relieve itself, it's probably not the puppy's fault. You could very well be responsible for contributing to the training's temporary failure. You may not be using the best techniques for your particular puppy, or may be inadvertently interrupting the puppy's toilet training in ways such as inconsistent rewards, meal times, or too infrequent outings. There are other things that can cause mistakes during potty training, from changes in diet and environment to medications and even vaccinations.

Dogs are not stubborn by nature. In fact, they are eager to please their owners by cooperating with training, including toilet training. They respond to the same stimuli as human children—praise, rewards, patience, understanding, and kindness. While some dogs are more intelligent than others, none are truly unable to learn when it comes to toilet training. It's not in the puppy's best interest to soil where it lives and eats. It's not in the puppy's nature to defy its owner on purpose or just for spite. What may seem to you as stubbornness may just be your puppy telling you it's not interested or engaged in the lessons. Try rewarding the pup more enthusiastically, either with better treats or a favorite game to get the puppy to be more attentive. As the saying goes, "if giving $10 isn't enough incentive, try $1000!"

There could be several reasons your friend is having trouble learning what you want. Review your training plan and schedule, and adjust them as necessary. Maybe the confined space is too large, or perhaps your puppy needs more frequent potty breaks. It could be that the area you are using is not appealing to the pup. Maybe it doesn't feel secure, or there is an odor it wishes to avoid. And make sure that you do not have unrealistic expectations of your pup to meet your needs. Instead, focus the training on you meeting the puppy's needs. With a little thoughtful review, you can find the answer and move forward.

Training a Puppy With Treats Is Bribery

Many people will withhold treats because they interpret them as spoiling or bribing the puppy. Think again. Training a puppy by giving treats when it performs properly is a means of positive reinforcement, one of the most important tools you have in your repertoire when it comes to teaching. Positive reinforcement plays on the natural instincts of a puppy to repeat behavior that is rewarded.

Treats are not the only way to give positive feedback, of course, although they are extremely effective. There are other rewards your puppy will respond to such as words of praise, physical touch, toys, or play sessions.

Rewards work, and that's the important thing. Human beings respond well to positive reinforcement too. At work a person responds well to words of praise from the boss or a raise in pay. Children in school are motivated when teachers give them stickers or special opportunities. It's no different with puppies.

All puppies will respond to positive reinforcement. There are apparently even some people who seem to believe that employing treats as training reinforcement works only with smaller breeds of dogs. The source of this idea is a mystery. Smaller dogs may have more difficulty learning good toilet training because their internal organs are small and liquid and solid waste goes "right through them." Therefore, they may need more reinforcement with both praise and more trips to the proper potty area. But rest assured, the same training methods work just as well for large and small breeds of dogs.

FAQ: Should I Rub My Puppy's Nose in Its Droppings?

No. This will not work in toilet training your puppy, for a number of reasons. In fact, it can be counterproductive.

First, puppies have a very short attention span. If you do not catch them in the act of soiling, they will not remember that they caused the mess. They will not recognize it as their own mistake. Rubbing their nose in feces or urine will not teach them anything positive, and may help instill fear of you.

This is not what negative reinforcement means. It should not be a way to punish your puppy for what are natural mistakes that happen in the process of toilet training. Negative reinforcement means not responding to the puppy when it does something wrong. Cleaning up and deodorizing the area without a fuss is the best way to respond. Or, if you catch the puppy "in the act," a firm word and bringing the pup to the correct area is sufficient.

What your puppy does learn when you rub its nose where it has relieved itself is that its owner punishes it at random, for no reason that the puppy can remember. This will confuse and frighten the puppy, which will cause it to distrust and fear its owner—exactly what you don't want the puppy to learn. Distrust and fear will carry over into other parts of your relationship with your puppy, making it difficult to train a puppy to be loyal, loving, and responsive to your needs and wishes. If you treat the puppy harshly and someone else in the household does not, it can come to prefer the other caregiver.

Chapter 6: Issues That Affect Toilet Training

Puppies don't stay puppies forever. They grow up into dogs—wonderful, well-behaved pets; that is, if their owners train and treat them right they do. You might think that toilet training your puppy ends after a few months. Certainly that's when the majority of the work is done. But there are still aspects you and your puppy can work on as it grows into an adult dog. Or, you may find yourself adopting an adult dog that needs to be toilet trained. Here's what you need to know.

Diet related habits, feeding patterns and environmental influences can certainly influence the toilet training process. Here are some common factors that new puppy owners have experienced:

- A change in diet. This can include switching from one type of food to another e.g dry to wet food, or switching to a different brand even if the formula is similar can take some getting used to. For some pups that check out fine medically, this new brand or that type of food just doesn't sit well with them. Some puppies do not tolerate lower-quality ingredients well. Check the ingredients list, and feed your puppy the best quality you can afford.

- A change in feeding routine.

o Changing the time, frequency and portions can greatly influence potty behavior and frequency. Pups, especially young ones, generally don't digest their food that well. It's common for pups to be fed too infrequently with portions that are too large. This can lead to indigestion and the problems that come with that. This is why at the beginning it's usually better to split the entire day's food into more meals. Four times a day is a minimum recommendation; for pups that are younger than 8 weeks, increase the frequency. As the pup matures, meals can become less frequent.

○ Keeping a consistent schedule is important, both in terms of meal times and subsequent outings. Inconsistent feeding times make it more difficult to predict when the pup will go. By observing how long it usually takes for the puppy to pee and poop after drinking or eating you can create a higher rate of success. Many owners become masters at predicting when their pup will go simply based on this.

● A combination of foods that just doesn't work. This usually applies more to those who prep their pup's food themselves. That particular ingredient or combination of ingredients just doesn't sit well for that puppy. Or it could be it is just the proportions/ratio of the ingredients that needs adjusting.

● A change in lifestyle or environment. Once pups are allowed to venture out more and explore different environments, it's inevitable they'll come into contact with some 'nasties'—bacteria, microbes, etc.—that affect their gut and may result in vomiting and/or diarrhea. Going to the beach seems to be a very common one, as dogs of any age new to this type of setting may be apt to ingest sand and salt water on the first few trips. Most eventually learn. If the pup is physically sound, usually the vomiting and diarrhea is short-lived. As always, *with any condition that is very severe or continues for two days or more, a veterinarian should be consulted immediately.*

● Grazers vs gobblers. Not all pups are gobblers, but for those that are, slowing down the feeding rate is recommended. Ingesting food too quickly, and often without even chewing, can result in vomiting. Adding water to the kibble, or putting stones or tennis balls in the feeding dish will make it more difficult for the puppy to wolf down large mouthfuls of food. Instead, they will have to pick around the obstacles which can slow things down a good bit. With grazers sometimes more vigilance is necessary to figure out their eating patterns.

If any of the above or, in particular, a combination of the above are consistently altered, it can be very difficult, if not impossible to identify the culprit(s). Therefore it is highly advisable to change things gradually and systematically, making it easier to assess the issues and figure out the necessary tweaks. It's important to note that these ideas are based on generalizations; toilet training issues are certainly not a 'one-size-fits-all' endeavor, and some experimenting is often necessary.

Toilet Training After One Year

Although some may consider a puppy to be an adult when it turns one year old, it is still young. In "dog years," it is the equivalent of a teenager, and it may still make many different kinds of mistakes. On the plus side, teenagers learn very quickly. They can also help their younger siblings learn the ropes. These older puppies can help you train younger ones by setting a good example.

Of course, it's best to toilet train before bad habits have time to become established. But let's assume you have done that. Why do you need to continue to toilet train?

For the most part, you can think of toilet training after one year as a refresher course. Your older puppy will have learned what is expected, but may need some reminding. As the puppy grows into an adult, it may yet have accidents and soil where you do not want it to.

Treat this the same as you would when a younger puppy breaks toilet training. Clean up the mess without any fuss and do not punish the dog. If, however, you catch it in the act, then you can say a firm 'no.' It is one word in the set of words dogs can come to understand. Dogs can and do understand the sound and meaning of words they are taught.

If your older puppy is well-trained it can exhibit that behavior for your younger puppy to emulate. Praise your grown pup for actions you want the younger one to copy, and both will benefit.

Older dogs may never have been toilet trained or may have forgotten their toileting lessons while living in unusual circumstances. If kept in kennels, for example, they may be used to soiling in their living spaces. In such cases, you may have to start from scratch with toilet training. Teaching an adult dog proper toilet etiquette is much like toilet training a puppy, but may take longer.

One thing that may help adult dogs learn to control their bladder and bowels is to recognize that there will be an adjustment period. During this time, it's a good idea to keep a journal of your dog's toileting habits. How often does it pee and how often does it poop? How long is it able to hold its waste? How often does it have accidents? What activity preceded the accidents? This will help you determine the rhythm of your dog's eliminations and what you need to do to intervene. It will also help you establish a toilet training routine, which is as essential for an adult dog as it is for puppies.

An adult dog has the muscular control to be able to hold its eliminations for up to ten hours. That means that your dog will likely not need a bathroom break during the night. It's best, though, to give your dog the opportunity to relieve itself much more often than that, every six hours or so and once more at bedtime—more often for a smaller breed of dog. Increase the time between potty breaks gradually.

Like puppies, adult dogs don't like to soil where they sleep, eat, or play. Use that to your advantage. Use a crate, baby gates, a dog playpen, or another barrier to give your dog a place that is its own for these non-toileting activities. Establish the out-of-doors as the proper place for toileting functions. If your dog is not used to going outside, you may want to use potty pads or even grass pads to get across the idea that the place for elimination is not within the house at large, but only in one location.

When you can't be around to watch your dog, have it stay in its special place. If you can be with the dog, pay attention to its signals that it may want to relieve itself, such as sniffing, pawing, whining, or lifting a leg or squatting. If the dog can go without soiling its area for approximately five days, it's time to increase the size of the area that it has as its own territory—a larger playpen or fenced area or a larger room, for example. If it has an accident, follow the standard clean-up procedure, including deodorizing.

Bad habits take more time to eliminate than good habits do to establish, so don't give up! Your adult dog is capable of learning toilet training with the same system of positive reinforcement for good behavior and a combination of patience, practice, and consistency.

Above: A beautiful litter of healthy puppies ready for their new homes.

Physical and Emotional Issues Can Affect Toilet Training

Physical issues such as urinary tract infections (UTIs), bladder or kidney disease, or gastrointestinal disorders can have an influence on whether your puppy has difficulty with toilet training. Changes in your puppy's diet, the presence of parasites, or even a seemingly harmless chewy treat can affect the digestive system, too. Or it can be one of a number of other health problems.

But did you know that puppies and dogs can have psychological issues that affect toilet training as well? Chief among these are stress and anxiety. These may be caused by being introduced to situations without proper acclimatization, or by certain events that create a change or a lack of security, as in separation anxiety. Both physical and psychological issues can lead to incontinence, and one may inadvertently create the other.

Anxiety: Its Effects and Prevention

Stress is created when your puppy undergoes an unpleasant situation such as being left alone or isolated for too long. Separation from its caregiver can also cause stress, as can excessive fear regarding various stimuli such as loud noises, being around people or other dogs, or new or strange experiences like riding in a car. Prolonged stress can turn into anxiety. It's normal for a puppy to feel some fear when first encountering these events, but if it doesn't gradually get used to such stimuli on its own, that response can grow into an anxiety disorder later in life. Fortunately, there are ways to prevent anxiety and treat it if it does occur.

Reading your pup's body language can help you prevent the development of anxiety that may lead to incontinence. This can also refer to your own body language. If you make threatening gestures or have body language indicating anger at your puppy's behavior, it can pick up on that and respond with fear. As mentioned earlier, fear can manifest in behaviors that may mask signs that your puppy needs to go. You should be able to observe bodily reactions in your puppy that indicate fear or anxiety. These can include: an increase in pottying mistakes, pacing, trembling, panting, excessive yawning, repetitive activity such as licking, or destructive behavior. Your puppy may also exhibit signs of avoidance, such as shrinking back or hiding in or behind its crate, or even away from you.

Treating Anxiety in Dogs

Pottying issues can make a puppy and its owner anxious. Those anxieties can create tummy problems. And tummy problems can make both puppy and owner anxious. It can be a difficult cycle to break. There are some things you can do that will help prevent your puppy from developing anxiety in the first place. These should start while your pet is still a puppy, and include using body language, socialization, obedience training, and situation avoidance.

If you suspect your puppy may be suffering from anxiety, you might try consulting with either a dog trainer or behavioral specialist, or a vet that has experience with diagnosing and fixing anxiety. Each may offer different solutions so a bit of research and trial-and-error may be necessary to see what fits best for your pup.

If you suspect physical causes are the reason behind incontinence you should consult your vet before investigating possible psychological problems.

Potential Health Issues

There are a number of diseases and disorders that can affect your puppy's toileting habits. Diabetes and chronic kidney disease, for example, can cause frequent urination. Ingesting toxic substances can result in loose stools, diarrhea, or even constipation. If you notice your puppy having to urinate more often than usual, or having persistent tummy trouble, you should take it to the vet right away.

Puppies may experience loose stools or diarrhea from time to time, and even constipation. These may be due to factors such as stress, changes in diet or exercise, the wrong food or treats, or by getting into something toxic. There are many plants that can cause gastrointestinal distress. Around your home and out in the world, your pup may ingest things it shouldn't. If you see blood in the urine or stool, or the problem persists for more than a day or so, you will again want to get your puppy to a veterinarian as soon as possible. The problem may be only a temporary one rather than a lifelong condition. But you'll want to know right away what you and the vet can do to make your puppy's life a long, healthy, and happy one.

People Foods and Other Things Not to Eat

There are many kinds of foods that puppies shouldn't eat, including among them some of the foods that you and your family eat. People food can upset your puppy's digestion since puppies have small and sensitive gastrointestinal tracts. For example, foods that are too rich or of poor quality can lead to a number of issues, such as constipation, diarrhea, gas, and other problems. Allergies to certain foods can create problems, too. One example is peanut butter. Many owners use peanut butter as a treat or a way to keep a puppy interested in and occupied with a toy. However, many dogs show sensitivity to certain foods. If you think something you are feeding him as either a meal or a treat could be creating toileting issues, change things up. You will find something that delights your dog and keeps its gut healthy.

There is also a condition called 'pica,' which can be responsible for puppies eating non-food substances including feces. Letting your puppy eat feces—their own or another animal's—is a bad idea, as poop can contain intestinal parasites that will affect its digestion or it may spread other diseases. This behavior usually stops after the puppy is about nine months old. Again, make sure that you keep the puppy's living area clean and do not place its feeding and toileting areas too close together.

Special Needs Dogs

Puppies don't have to be physically perfect to be the perfect pet for you. Many people open their hearts and homes to dogs with disabilities and are repaid with loyalty, love, and joy. You may have adopted one of these special needs dogs from a shelter, or a puppy you already share your life with may become disabled as it ages. Either way, you and your canine companion can still live a happy, fulfilled life together.

Are puppies with special needs too difficult to train at all? Certainly not. It may require a little bit of imagination and innovation, but it is certainly doable. You'll find that training a puppy with special needs relies on the same basic principles as training an able-bodied pup. Often, all that is needed are a few adaptations.

Deaf Dogs

One difficulty in training deaf puppies is that they don't respond to the verbal cues that you may be used to giving a puppy. You may tell a deaf pup, "it's time to go out" as a signal, or say "good dog!" or click a clicker for positive reinforcement, and yet those forms of reinforcement will be futile; you will not be able to use sounds such as your voice as positive reinforcement. That doesn't mean that a deaf dog can't be trained, though. It does mean that you will have to use the puppy's other senses—and a little ingenuity—to replace verbal signals with communication through the other senses.

Communication with a deaf puppy requires using its senses of smell, sight, and touch to provide instruction and reinforcement. Sense of smell is especially keen in dogs. Puppies often use their noses to determine where to relieve themselves. This is what makes it so difficult to house train a puppy if you do not thoroughly clean and deodorize a spot where it has soiled.

Scent is also used to mark where the puppy is supposed to go. If you make sure that the puppy scent-marks only in approved toileting spaces, you will have gone a long way in ensuring that your puppy gets the right idea. In addition, scent can be used to direct a puppy to the right spot. For example, you can direct your puppy by laying out a line of treats leading to the designated area.

Puppies also rely on sight to communicate with their owners. They can read their owners' facial expressions and body language. A brief frown, headshake, or wagging finger can convey the word 'no' to a puppy, while it can learn that a smile and/or a thumbs-up means 'yes' or 'good.' You want to make good, positive eye contact with your puppy, so be sure not to glare at it when it makes a mistake.

It's possible to train a puppy to respond to a variety of hand signals such as ones for 'sit' or 'stay.' Puppies can also learn to recognize a vocabulary of hand signals related to toileting, and can even learn to understand simple commands given in American Sign Language (ASL). After the puppy has arrived at its toileting location, you give it an appropriate hand signal, followed by a reward when it performs correctly. That positive reinforcement can come from a treat or a hand signal showing approval.

Using physical touch is important for all dogs. They like being stroked, or scratched on the back or belly. Using touch as both a way to get a deaf puppy's attention and to give it praise will be greatly appreciated. And, of course, don't forget the treats!

If you need to get a deaf puppy's attention, you can flick the lights if you are indoors or toss a stick in front of it outdoors. Or you can tap the puppy on the back. When the puppy gives you its attention, give a reward that will serve to reinforce the behavior.

Blind Dogs

Puppies may become blind due to accidents or illness, or may simply be born blind or with limited vision. You therefore must rely on a blind puppy's senses of hearing, smell, and touch in order to accomplish potty training.

Proceed with scent training the same as described for a deaf dog—or indeed for any puppy. And replace visual cues with verbal ones. Since puppies can learn to understand over 100 different words, you have plenty of flexibility to teach commands such as 'slow' or 'easy' for slower walking and 'stop' if there is a hazard in the way. All other aspects of toilet training still apply here; treats, touch and praise are all forms of positive reinforcement that work with blind puppies.

Using a trail of treats to guide the pup to its crate or sleeping area will help it quickly learn to identify that location. A blind puppy can also learn its way around the house and even be able to manage stairs, but it may help to put bells on the collars of other pets so it can keep track of their location.

A puppy that is both blind and deaf is more difficult to train, but it can still be accomplished with a combination of scent, touch, treats—and lots of patience and repetition.

Your Mobility-Challenged Puppy

Mobility-challenged puppies and dogs sometimes use the doggie equivalent of wheelchairs—carts that support their back legs while their front legs provide the power. Although puppies can get around just fine on three legs, a cart will allow them to be more mobile if they have lost the use of two legs. And have no fear—puppies that use a mobility device are able to relieve themselves between the back wheels, and won't hesitate to learn to do so.

Your puppy will also need special treatment when it is recovering from surgery. You may have to carry it to the toileting area for a while so that it won't forget its toilet training while limited in mobility.

Chapter 7: Other Potty Training Issues

It's vitally important to monitor as much of your puppy's activities as possible, and make sure to keep its surroundings clean and free from potential hazards, like household cleaners, or toxic house or garden plants. By paying close attention to the pup's activity, you may more easily recall what might have precipitated an accident.

Here are some hazards to watch out for, many of which can involve your puppy's bowel and bladder health and so affect toilet training.

Poisons and Toxins

There are many substances that your puppy should not eat because they are poisonous or toxic to growing dogs as well as adult ones. Common houseplants, including holiday plants such as mistletoe, holly, and poinsettias and some outdoor plants, like yew and azalea, are very toxic to pets. And puppies are prone to mischief! You may have to reorganize plants and protect certain yard areas for your puppy's first year to keep it safe.

Household cleaners, automotive products, and other substances, such as mouse and rat bait, are also highly toxic and even deadly. Puppy-proof your home and yard the same way you would for a child. If you suspect that your puppy's accidents may be due to some kind of toxic substance, bring the pup to the vet right away! If treated quickly, many toxic poisonings can be dealt with.

Fleas, Ticks, and Other Pests

Fleas and ticks can spread harmful diseases to your puppy, including ones that can affect its bowel habits. Internal parasites, or 'worms,' can create digestive and nutrition issues. Fleas can transmit tapeworms to your dog, and other things your pup may get into while out in the yard or walking through town may transfer a variety of parasites, as well. Even if your puppy stays indoors all the time and uses potty pads, fleas and ticks can still enter your household via visitors, their dogs, or your own clothing.

The Breeder as a Resource

There may be other difficulties that arise while toilet training your puppy. Sometimes it can be helpful to know more about where your puppy came from and what its experiences have been. The pup's parents or perhaps other littermates may have had similar issues. If you got your puppy from a reliable source, such as a breeder, you may find some answers there.

A good puppy breeder can be an invaluable source of information. They can make all the difference in ensuring that your puppy is healthy and happy—and prepared for toilet training. The breeder may even have already begun the toilet training process once the puppy reached an appropriate age. If this is the case—and lucky you, if it is— you will want to ask a lot of questions as to how the breeder has gone about the training, e.g., what tools and methods did they use, what type of set-up is there, and has the training been mostly inside or outside, or both? Breeders are generally very proud of their dogs, and want them to go to good homes who will train them properly and keep them happy and healthy. Don't feel as if you are bothering them with questions about potty training; they want you and the puppy to be glad that you found each other!

Occasionally, even puppies that come from a shelter or adoption organization may have started toilet training, either while at the shelter or from a previous owner. While it may take a pup that has been through the shelter experience a while to gain trust and feel secure, they should still be very trainable.

One thing to ask of a breeder, seller, or individual from whom you get your new friend is about its vaccination records. This is especially important if you will be bringing the puppy into a home with other pets, or before you begin socializing with other dogs while out walking or playing. Ask the breeder whether the puppy has been given the appropriate shots, and to see the puppy's health records. The breeder should be able to provide you with these. Good breeders, whether professional or amateur, love to chat about puppies and help their new owners learn as much as possible. Asking a breeder questions about the puppy's breed, littermates, and parents will give you a lot of information about your new pet.

Profile: Percy's Pooping Problems

Percy was an almost perfect puppy in so many ways. Sociable, playful, and great with kids and other animals (except squirrels). By fifteen weeks old, Percy knew where to pee, and, just as importantly, where *not* to pee. Percy slept all night, so there was no longer any need for midnight outings. The only issue Percy had was pooping. This seemed to happen anywhere and at anytime, regardless of meal times.

Although Percy kept the kennel clean, the rest of the designated area was fair game, as was the hallway leading to the door and the front walk. Unlike most other dogs, Percy did not have a particular area of the yard preferred for bowel movements. The whole yard was a mess of soft poo.

After trying several different foods over a period of time with no improvement, and even after consulting with the vet, the reason for Percy's behavior remained a mystery. Only once the new owners contacted the breeder did the issue become clear: Percy's parents both developed canine Irritable Bowel Disease, or IBD, as they grew older. It seems poor Percy, as a result, was born with it.

Armed with this new information, Percy's owners consulted again with their veterinarian, who prescribed a special food designed specifically for treating and supporting dogs with IBD. A few weeks after changing to the recommended food, Percy was a perfectly potty-trained pooch!

FAQ: Why Is Understanding Commands Important?

The principles you use for toilet training, such as positive reinforcement and verbal commands, can be used for teaching puppies other lessons as well. Your puppy has the ability to learn up to 200 words, so in addition to toileting commands and reinforcements like "time to go out" or "time for a walk," "good dog," and variations of praise, you can teach your puppy a number of other actions. Other common commands that new owners want to teach puppies include sit, stay, no, and lie down. These can be vital in ensuring your puppy is safe and healthy.

As with any training, consistency is key. Once you have decided on the words and actions (e.g., hand gestures) you want to use, stick with them. Your puppy will make the connection between the word, action, and affect much more quickly than if you use a different phrase each time.

When you take your puppy outdoors for relieving itself, it may try to run into a busy street, or simply put its nose where it doesn't belong, like a neighbor's yard. These are examples of why it is essential that your puppy learns the word 'no.' The same is true if they try to approach people or other dogs you encounter on the way. By using the leash and your leash training in conjunction with the verbal command, the puppy will get the idea that it is not allowed to roam and explore at will.

When teaching any of these commands, positive reinforcement is again employed. For example, if you want the puppy to sit, give the verbal command and gently push the puppy's rump to the ground while raising its head or holding a treat above its nose. Once the pup sits—even for a moment—it is time to give the puppy praise and the treat for obeying. Gradually increase the amount of time your puppy must stay in 'sit' before getting the rewards, keeping in mind that puppies still have a very short attention span. You aren't looking for long stretches at first. Even a few moments can make a puppy more settled and refocus their attention. Eventually, your puppy will respond to the verbal command alone.

This command can be useful in a number of circumstances—for example, when you are walking your puppy in a city and need to cross a street. If your puppy can sit quietly by your feet while waiting for the light to change, your walks will be both more pleasant and safer. The commands to stay, heel, and wait will also be of help in similar situations. Asking your dog to sit or wait before leashing can help prevent accidents from an over-excited puppy that is allowed to jump around in preparation for a potty outing.

Above: A puppy shows off an exemplary sit. Notice how calm and attentive the pup is.

A Tale of an Excited Puppy

Señor Sanchez was adored by the whole family since arriving as an eight-week old puppy. Yet at twice that age, and although consistently keeping the designated area and the whole house accident-free, as well as asking clearly when going outside was needed, the pup would still have accidents, generally peeing when waiting to be leashed for a walk. And leashing Sanchez could take a while; the puppy would become so excited it was difficult to snap the lead to the collar as the ball of fluff jumped and twisted. How could they get this pup to settle down—and avoid peeing from excitement and stimulation—when getting ready for a walk?

This example shows the benefits to teaching at least simple commands to your pup, starting at an early age. Although the puppy won't "get it" right away, just as with potty training repetition and consistency coupled with rewards and praise will get them there much more quickly.

Sanchez's family began teaching the puppy to sit, wait, and lie down. They taught these things separately from the excitement of feeding and walk times. Over time, their consistency and use of lots of praise and rewards, the puppy began to perform all those things on command. Once established, the family could now ask Sanchez to 'sit' when getting the lead clipped, and to 'wait' while the door was opened. If the pup was particularly squirmy that day, "lie down" would not only help with settling, it would also prevent a peeing accident.

By keeping Señor Sanchez's attention on the owner and the commands, the excitement was lowered, and the pup could stay calm while waiting to go outside to do business. Asking for the puppy's attention to be on the given command switched its focus away from the door and onto the person in a calm and engaging way. Teaching the commands had the added benefits of preparing Sanchez for future obedience training, and could be used when walking to help deflate an exciting interaction, be it another person, puppy, or squirrel.

TOILET TRAINING YOUR PUPPY

Chapter 8: Common Problems and Ways to Fix Them

There are a number of problems that new owners have when it comes to toilet training a new puppy. Many of these involve the location where it sleeps and where it performs toileting functions. Of course, it's best to keep these areas separate if at all possible. Here are some examples of a puppy's unclean behavior, some reasons why it may occur, and steps you can take to correct it.

FAQ: How Do I Clean Poopy Puppy Fur

In general, your puppy's habits and anatomy will mean that regular cleaning of the area under its tail is not a daily task. While wiping your dog's bottom may not be necessary there are ways that puppies occasionally can't avoid getting some fecal matter stuck in the fur. This can happen particularly—but not only—in breeds with long or curly hair, drooping tails (rather than erect tails), or when the stools are loose. There are a few tricks you can use to gently clean your dog's bottom.

Trim the fur to keep it short. Long hair around the anus can trap poop even if it is only a little soft, as can curly hair. Keeping the area trimmed will reduce that issue tremendously. The same goes for the fur under the base of the tail—a place where many dog owners forget to look.

When feces is present, use a warm, damp cloth or towel and a gentle stroking or circular motion to loosen and remove as much poop as you can without pulling hair or scrubbing. You don't want your puppy to dislike the process!

A tiny bit of doggy soap or shampoo can help break up the fecal matter, making it easier to wipe away. For any material stuck in the hair, use a fine-toothed comb and some fur detangler to make sure all the dried, stuck bits are gone. Again, remember to check under the tail, too.

Puppy wipes are available that will take the place of the damp cloth and gentle cleanser. Never use baby wipes; most commercially available brands contain ingredients that are toxic to dogs, such as propylene glycol. Alcohol-based wipes, if used frequently, can cause dryness, which will in turn create irritation.

Sometimes a puppy may develop the unusual habit of rolling in its own, or more commonly another dog's feces. This is a behavior that you can remedy quite effectively in two ways. One is by teaching your puppy to 'leave it' while guiding or moving it away from the offensive matter. The other is by keeping the designated space and the yard tidy, disposing of waste frequently and properly, e.g., disinfecting to remove odors.

Once the deed has been done, you can neutralize odors quickly by using baking soda sprinkled on the messy areas, then follow up using the same methods as above if the mess is small. For a larger issue, a full bath may be necessary.

Sleeping and Peeing
Leslie's Story

"My puppy sleeps on the toilet area of its crate," Leslie says. "And it pees on the sleeping surface. Why does it do this and what can I do?"

There are several reasons Leslie's puppy may be doing this. It may be because the toilet area is more comfortable to sleep on. If the puppy is frequently changing sleeping locations it's often looking for somewhere more comfortable to sleep. There needs to be a bigger distinction between the toilet area and the sleeping area. The sleeping area clearly needs to be a more attractive option for sleeping.

Thermal comfort is key. Because the pee pad may be cooler and the sleeping surface too hot, the pee pad may be the most attractive option to sleep on even when soiled. Sometimes pups flip-flop between the toilet area and bed. They can't seem to get comfortable or remain comfortable for long. This usually happens in warmer climates and environments, or during a change in seasons. The location of your puppy's crate or other confined space can also play a significant role. Is it in a very warm part of the house? Does the toilet area lie directly in the sun during part of the day?

Try to make the sleeping surface cooler. Experiment with different types of materials, location of the crate or confined space, and cooling areas such as near a fan or air conditioner. In warmer climates or conditions, puppies often prefer to lie on tiles or wood rather than fabric. Or you might move the location of the confined space to a cooler part of the house. Perhaps you can set up multiple confined spaces or toilet areas throughout the house or apartment.

Another possibility is that the bed smells like pee. After all, you wouldn't want to sleep in a location that smells like a toilet either! Dogs are often drawn to surfaces that smell of urine. If the bed has been soiled heavily or frequently, it may be necessary to discard it altogether. It can be difficult or impossible to get the smell out completely, no matter how many times it's been washed or what type of cleaning agent you use. (You might try white vinegar in the wash cycle and see if that works.)

Your puppy may be seeking attention. This can be caused by not getting rewarded for proper toilet behavior, particularly for very young pups. It may be unclear to the pup that there will be a reward for peeing in the proper location or the reward isn't one that the puppy prefers. Does your puppy prefer edible treats or words of praise and a pat on the head? Find out what your puppy likes best and give it that for good toileting behavior. Be generous with praise and/or treats. Especially with young puppies it's important to consistently reward them for going in the right spot. Very young pups may not yet be able to make the connection that rewards are given for toileting in the right location.

Puppies can also get bored or frustrated. It's not ideal for puppies to spend a lot of time in confined spaces when they are wide awake and full of energy. Vigorous play can lead to the need to relieve themselves. You should take your puppy to the proper toileting location after a play session.

Ron's Story

Ron complains, "My puppy both sleeps and pees in its toileting area!"

A possible reason for this not-uncommon behavior is that the pup may never have learned from a young age to differentiate between the two locations. Typically, pups bred at puppy mills have been forced to pee and poop where they sleep. Or a stray puppy that you adopt may have learned toileting behavior from a mother who was untrained herself.

Over time, if the toilet area is consistently kept clean and the dog is consistently guided as to where the designated area is, it will usually develop hygienic habits. More patience with the dog can lead to vast improvement. It needs to be guided more frequently to the right spot and rewarded.

Make the toilet area a less attractive option to sleep on. Make it physically less comfortable to sleep on by adding objects that would make the toileting areas uncomfortable to lie on, for example sticks or stones. Or use a different material such as artificial grass dog latrines. Some are designed to be a little bit prickly and therefore uncomfortable to lie on.

Use odors to your advantage. Apply an artificial odor on the toilet surface that signals to the dog this is the toilet area. This strategy works for some dogs. You may need to experiment a little with different odor formulas.

Though it's admittedly an unusual strategy, sometimes using two pee pads can work— one as the sleeping surface and the other as the toilet. By simply placing some of the puppy's urine on one of the pee pads, it may naturally use that as the toilet and sleep on the clean pee pad. Understand, however, that young puppies can get easily confused. Be consistent with the location of potty pads that are used as the toilet and sleeping surface. For example, the pad on the right could always be the designated toilet area and the one on the left for sleeping.

Knowing Where To Go
Kim's Story

Kim reports that, "My puppy soils everywhere within its crate. What do the puppy experts say?"

This may be because it's simply unclear to the puppy where to go. Kim has not been able to make a clear enough distinction between sleeping surface and toilet area. Gently guide the pup to the correct location, then reward it generously and consistently when it performs its toileting functions where it's supposed to.

It could also be that the toilet area is not being cleaned up frequently enough to meet the puppy's standards. Clean the area thoroughly and regularly. Most dogs will urinate on a pee pad three to five times before it becomes too smelly to use again. Many dogs won't go back to poop unless it's been cleaned up. Some dogs can be very finicky; even after urinating one time they won't go back.

The confined space or crate may be too small and the sleeping surface and toilet area overlap. When the puppy lies down or when it soils, it accidentally does so on the sleeping surface. It just becomes one big toilet.

A simple, easy way to stop this behavior is to increase the size of the confined space. Remember the general rule: the minimum size should be three times the length of the puppy, and one and a half times as wide.

Tom's Story

Tom says, "My puppy soils both inside and outside its contained space. Why does this happen?"

The puppy has likely been given too much freedom and space to decide where to go. Again, the size of the confined space matters. It should essentially contain only two surface areas, the sleeping surface and the toilet surface. The sleeping surface should just be large enough so the dog can completely sprawl out, turn around, and sleep comfortably without coming into contact with the toilet surface. The toilet area needs to be big enough so the dog can move, turn around, and pee and poop comfortably. With only two types of surface areas, the puppy is forced to make a choice. If you get the sleeping surface right, then your puppy will naturally perform its toileting on the other surface, which has no value to it.

Or it may be that the location of the crate is wrong—too far away from where the puppy's humans are spending most of their time. Puppies want to be close to their 'pack.' If the toileting area is too far away from where all the activity is, either the puppy won't get there in time or when it does, the owners are unable to get there quickly enough to give a meaningful reward. If the confined space is concealed from view, the owner may not even be aware that the pup has used the wrong space for toileting.

Another issue may be that you have been rewarding the puppy inconsistently and/or not generously enough. Make sure the puppy is very aware when it has done the right thing—throw that puppy party! And, as always, don't make a big deal of it when the puppy makes a mistake. Just clean the problem area calmly and thoroughly without getting angry or letting the puppy know that you are upset.

Many times, the reason a puppy continues to make mistakes can be traced back to the set-up, the condition of its designated space, or the consistency in the training and feeding schedule. Often there are multiple factors in play. Another often overlooked element is lack of play and exercise. Besides keeping a growing pup happy and healthy, regular play sessions (more than once a day) and walks help keep the pup's insides regular, too. Just as for people, puppy's need both mental and physical stimulation to keep all systems working optimally. If your puppy is too confined, it may not be able to develop a regular routine for pottying, and it may also learn that, by going where it shouldn't, it will get the owner's attention and be taken outside!

A Tale of Two Dachshunds

Dan and Janet had a more complicated problem. Their two dachshunds, Toby and Louise, who were seven months old, had a confined space that was a playpen which they both occupied. There was a separate bed for each of the puppies. But they soiled anywhere inside the playpen, not seeming to care whether it was on the potty pads, on the beds, or elsewhere. Each morning, there was a big mess to clean up. The owners had no idea which dog was the problem or if neither one knew how to use the toilet area properly. They tried washing the beds, but it seemed to have no effect. The puppies just couldn't seem to get the right idea. They had to combine a number of solutions in order to correct the problem.

The first was the matter of thermal comfort. The problem began to arise during the hot part of the year, and the playpen was located in the warmest part of the house, near a window that let direct sunlight into the puppies' confined space. The dogs weren't comfortable sleeping on their beds, so they did not consider the beds "off limits" as they would have a crate or den space, and did their toileting anywhere in the confined space.

The owners moved the playpen to an area directly under the air conditioner and set up another confined space in a tiled area of the apartment where the dogs could choose to sleep at night. This was one part of solving the problem.

But there were other issues as well. Dan and Janet had no idea whether it was Toby or Louise (or both of them) causing the difficulty. With both of them sharing the playpen, it just wasn't clear.

The solution to this was fairly easy. They could have gotten a separate playpen for each dog. Instead they used a divider to section off two separate areas of the confined space. When the puppies indicated a need to go, the owners put them in the playpen and observed.

It quickly became clear that Toby basically had the right idea while Louise was making most of the mistakes. The owners' goal was to have both of the puppies consistently doing their toileting on the potty pads and not on the beds.

The beds themselves were part of the problem. They had been used for toileting so often that they retained the smell and made it seem to the puppies that the beds were an okay place to defecate and urinate. This confusion led to them soiling the beds on many occasions. The potty pads were also problematic. They were not changed often enough and were unpleasant to use, so the dogs sought other areas to relieve themselves.

Cleaning the beds had no effect. The truth was that simply cleaning the beds was not sufficient. Even though they smelled better to the owners, they didn't to Toby and Louise! Dan and Janet had to buy new beds for the pups. Within five days, Toby was using the beds appropriately—for sleeping at least—and he understood the different areas right away. Louise still toileted both on the potty pads, which were cleaned more often and on other surfaces in the playpen areas, though she did seem to prefer sleeping on her new bed.

Another difficulty was the lack of consistency in rewarding the puppies for proper toileting behavior. When they went on the potty pads, the owners should have given positive reinforcement—and generously. But Dan and Janet both worked during the day, giving Toby and Louise the opportunity—and the space—to go wherever they wanted. Since Toby got the idea fairly quickly, it was Louise who needed the best incentives. Toilet training her required the 'million-dollar' reward—the treat or toy she liked best, plus extravagant praise.

It took ten days before both of the puppies figured out that soiling only on the potty pads was the best option. Still, they continued to soil in various areas of the playpen, not just where they were supposed to. Dan and Janet began to notice when Toby and Louise were about to relieve themselves, and placed them in the playpen where they could use the potty pads. That was a good idea, but it didn't solve the whole problem.

The owners' goal was to have the puppies perform their toileting functions outdoors rather than in the apartment. But Dan and Janet both worked all day and were not on hand to supervise Toby and Louise. In addition, their apartment was on the fifth floor, so to reach the outdoor toileting area (a nearby gutter that was convenient for the owners to use disposable bags to clean up the mess) they had to go downstairs in the elevator and across the lobby. This was too long for the young puppies to hold their bowels and especially their bladders.

Because of their work schedules, Dan and Janet were only able to take the puppies out two times a day, instead of the at least four times that they needed. Employing a dog-walker to take them outside a couple of extra times per day proved to be a good solution. In about five weeks, Toby and Louise were fully trained; they were old enough to hold on until taken out, so they no longer needed the potty pads, and they both learned that they should wait to be taken outside to relieve themselves.

In all, Dan and Janet were doing many things wrong, which led to the puppies having trouble meeting expectations for proper toileting habits. First, they couldn't tell which puppy presented the bigger problem. The playpen where the puppies slept was in the wrong location. The beds were not hygienic enough to suit Toby and Louise, so they thought they were a proper place to use for toileting. Lack of consistency also hindered the owners' efforts, both in supervising the puppies during the day and in giving them sufficient rewards when they did their toileting in the right place. Dan and Janet's absence during the day and the long way from their apartment to the outside left Toby and Louise unsupervised for much of the day. It's no wonder that the puppies presented a variety of toileting problems!

Gradually, the owners worked through their problems and their puppies learned what was expected of them. It took a few additional months until they were fully trained and didn't make any more mistakes; in the end, it was worth taking the time to get to the real issue. By adding more time and additional training, both dogs became the super citizens their owners wanted. Putting in place all the remedies, along with consistency and patience, made the biggest difference.

Conclusion

Toilet training your new puppy may have seemed like an impossible task when you first came home with your new friend. With patience, consistency, repetition—and lots of treats—you did it! I hope this book has helped you with the process and that now you and your puppy are ready for a long and happy life together. Toilet training is only the first step in that adventure.

There are many commands and behaviors you will want to teach your puppy. Of course, toilet training is the subject that most new puppy owners want to tackle first. It can be very unpleasant to live in a household where the puppy hasn't been toilet trained thoroughly and consistently. Adding other commands to training such as 'sit' or 'stay' can actually help you accomplish your toilet training goals. They can deepen your relationship, and teach your puppy to listen. Certain commands will also help teach it to have patience, whether getting ready to go outside, or when out walking on a leash.

Once your puppy is toilet trained, though, you will be able to spend more quality time together, both indoors and outdoors. Monitoring your puppy's toileting habits won't be a chore anymore. Teaching the puppy where and when to relieve itself has allowed you to move on to more pleasurable pursuits such as playing fetch or Frisbee. And if your puppy does make occasional mistakes, you now know how to handle them with a minimum of fuss and distress to both you and the puppy.

A properly toilet trained puppy is a great companion for people of all ages and in all sorts of living arrangements. Just because you live in an apartment, for example, or share your house with children doesn't mean that having a puppy isn't a possibility for you. Puppies are quite adaptable, and if their owners are, too, toilet training a puppy should go smoothly and lead to years of happy companionship.

About the Author

James Leung is a professional member of the Association of Professional Dog Trainers. He specializes in pet obedience and behavior modification, helping dogs and owners make the necessary adjustments to achieve a more harmonious balance. James uses a combination of positive reinforcement and proven training methods to create a balanced training system that fosters the desired behavior. His techniques are tailored to suit the needs of both the dog and owner. James understands clear communication between handler and dog is essential to achieve the desired results. He firmly believes training should be enjoyed by both dog and owner for the best outcome.

Glossary

AKC (American Kennel Club)—organization that registers dogs and provides information on dog behavior and training

Breeder—business that offers puppies from registered or purebred dogs for sale

Clicker—training aid; a small plastic device that emits a clicking sound

Confined Space—crate, playpen, or other space used for training puppy

Negative Reinforcement—removing a stimulus to condition a puppy not to perform an action

Pheromones—natural substances produced by the body that a puppy can smell

Positive Reinforcement—rewarding a puppy with treats, praise, or play for performing an action correctly

Thundershirt—type of harness that fits closely and reduces anxiety in a puppy

Image References

Fewings, N. (2021, May 2). *Cockapoo puppy sitting* [Image]. Unsplash. *nick-fewings-RCz6eSVPGYU-unsplash.*

Gorelova, T. (2020, September 11). *Puppy chewing fabric* [Image]. Pexels. *pexels-tanya-gorelova-3860308.jpg*

Im, T. (2018, April 20). *Two Dachshunds* [Image]. Pexels. *pexels-tatiana-lm-976921.jpg.*

Katt, S. (2020, August 22). *Puppy in harness* [Image]. Pexels. *pexels-samson-katt-5255554.jpg.*

Kievskaya, D. (2018, March 25). *Pug puppy pulling rope toy* [Image]. Pexels. *pexels-anna-shvets-4587991.jpg.*

Mangulsone, K. (2015, December 22). *Real life best friends* [Image]. Unsplash. *unsplash.com/photos/9gz3wfHr65U*

Neizkasha, M. (n.d.). *Puppy chewing* [Image]. Pexels. *pexels-margo-neizhkasha-12008468.jpg.*

Neumeyer, J. (2018, February 20). *Eurasier litter in basket* [Image]. Unslpash. *judi-neumeyer-ECjHeJtRznQ-unsplash.jpg.*

Singh, Y. (2020, August 29). *Owner with puppy* [Image]. Unsplash. *yogendra-singh-K8JxScoZb4A-unsplash.jpg.*

Verschueren, A. (2022, January 20). *Peeing puppy* [Image]. Unsplash. *unsplash.com/photos/BcQQZ0B9d1s*

Verschueren, A. (n.d.). *Dog in crate* [Image]. Unsplash. *ayla-verschueren-qvbG3-tZnyc-unsplash.jpg.*

Verschueren, A. (2022, August 8). *Puppy in grass* [Image]. Unsplash. *ayla-verschueren-BcQQZ0B9d1s-unsplash.jpg.*

References

Bovsun, M. (2019, March 2). *How to Potty Train a Puppy: A Comprehensive Guide for Success.* American Kennel Club; American Kennel Club. https://www.akc.org/expert-advice/training/how-to-potty-train-a-puppy/

Burke, A. (2016, November 29). *American Kennel Club.* American Kennel Club. https://www.akc.org/expert-advice/health/treating-dog-anxiety/

Guest Post: The Do's and Don'ts of Potty Training a Puppy. (2017, July 13). Pete the Vet. https://www.petethevet.com/guest-post-the-dos-and-donts-of-potty-training-a-puppy/

House Training Your Puppy | VCA Animal Hospitals. (n.d.). Vcahospitals.com. Retrieved May 12, 2022, from https://vcahospitals.com/know-your-pet/house-training-your-puppy

How to get your dog to stop barking. (2020). The Humane Society of the United States. https://www.humanesociety.org/resources/how-get-your-dog-stop-barking

How to Potty Train an Adult Dog. (n.d.). www.preventivevet.com. https://www.preventivevet.com/dogs/how-to-potty-train-an-adult-dog

Medical Conditions That Might Be Hindering Puppy's Potty Training. (2021, July 17). How to Potty Train a Puppy. https://howtopottytrainapuppy.net/medical-conditions-hindering-puppys-potty-training/

Poisonous Plants for Dogs. (n.d.). Www.petmd.com. Retrieved May 12, 2022, from https://www.petmd.com/dog/emergency/poisoning-toxicity/e_dg_poisonous_plants

Poisons (Swallowed). (n.d.). Www.petmd.com. Retrieved May 12, 2022, from https://www.petmd.com/dog/emergency/poisoning-toxicity/e_dg_swallowed_poisons

Puppy Development: Stages from Birth to Two Years Old. (2018). Best Friends Animal Society. https://resources.bestfriends.org/article/puppy-development-stages-birth-two-years-old

Tamisiea, J. (n.d.). *Dogs' Personalities Aren't Determined by Their Breed.* Scientific American. Retrieved May 12, 2022, from https://www.scientificamerican.com/article/dogs-personalities-arent-determined-by-their-breed/

Tips for Housetraining Your Puppy. (n.d.). WebMD. https://pets.webmd.com/dogs/guide/house-training-your-puppy

Tips for Training the Special Needs Dog. (2008, March 6). Dog Star Daily. https://www.dogstardaily.com/blogs/tips-training-special-needs-dog

Top Potty Training Sprays (Of 15 Tested!) (2022) DogLab https://DogLab.com/potty-training-spray

Understanding Why Dogs Bark. (n.d.). WebMD. https://pets.webmd.com/dogs/guide/understanding-why-dogs-bark

What to Expect: Introducing a Puppy to Your Adult Dogs | Karen Pryor Clicker Training. (2013, August 1). Www.clickertraining.com. https://www.clickertraining.com/what-to-expect-introducing-a-puppy-to-your-adult-dogs

Don't miss out!

Visit the website below and you can sign up to receive emails whenever James Leung publishes a new book. There's no charge and no obligation.

https://books2read.com/r/B-A-ZXKV-XZDCC

BOOKS2READ

Connecting independent readers to independent writers.